The Artist Blacksmith

The Artist Blacksmith

Design and Techniques

Peter Parkinson

The Crowood Press

First published in 2001 by
The Crowood Press Ltd
Ramsbury, Marlborough
Wiltshire SN8 2HR

www.crowood.com

This impression 2010

British Library Cataloguing-in-Publication Data
A catalogue record for this book is available from the British Library.

ISBN 978 1 86126 428 2

Dedication
I would like to thank all those blacksmiths who have generously lent me illustrations and countless more whose advice and enthusiasm, whether they know it or not, has contributed to this book.

Photographic Acknowledgements
All photographs by the author with the exception of those credited otherwise, and the following: Peter Hill 76 (bottom); Andrew Lee 83; Ian Macaulay 84, 85 (top), 101 (top); Paul Taylor 89 (top).

Line drawings by the author.

PREVIOUS PAGE: containers and forged mild steel twigs by the author. Containers made from mild steel angle section, cut and hot folded to trap the base in slots, with cut and punched decoration.

Please Note
I have tried where possible throughout this book to use gender neutral words, in the knowledge that blacksmithing is by no means a male preserve. I have nevertheless used 'he' and 'his', because to add 'she' and 'hers' every time would become unbearably tedious. If this still rankles, I can only apologize and emphasize that 'he' is simply a pronoun, and not intended as an opinion.

Typefaces used: Plantin (main text and headings), Helvetica (labels).

Typeset and designed by
D & N Publishing
Baydon, Marlborough, Wiltshire.

Printed and bound in Malaysia by Times Offset (M) Sdn. Bhd.

CONTENTS

INTRODUCTION

Blacksmithing has come a long way in the last twenty years. In 1979 I was invited as a guest to the Crafts Council Forging Iron Conference and Workshop at Hereford, organized with the intention of revitalizing an apparently dying craft. The main participants were fourteen blacksmiths from all over Britain, many of whom had never met before and had been under the impression that they were the last real blacksmith in the country.

Since that time the craft has expanded dramatically, developed artistically, embraced new technologies and found new applications. Blacksmithing has been taught in a number of Art Colleges since 1982. The British Artist Blacksmiths Association – BABA – founded in 1978, now has some 600 members, amateur and professional, and a thriving annual programme of events. Perhaps surprisingly there is also a significant international dimension to the craft, providing a very active and fertile network between smiths in America, Europe, Russia, Japan and Australia.

Typical BABA blacksmithing event.

Despite its increasing sophistication, blacksmithing has not forgotten its roots. The heart of modern blacksmithing is still the fire, the anvil and the hammer. You heat the metal and shape it with a hammer. The core activity of the smith today would be easily recognized and understood by a smith transported, for example, from medieval times.

On my shelf is a book published to accompany the 1980 British Museum exhibition, 'The Vikings', that includes a photograph of a group of tools left in the grave of a tenth-century Norwegian weapon-smith. The tongs, hammers and chisels are virtually identical to tools I use in my workshop today, a whole millennium later.

At that time iron was an expensive metal, difficult to produce in any quantity and valued for its use in tools and weaponry, implements and even jewellery. The smith made his own tools and would save and rework metal, welding small pieces together to make a larger bar if necessary.

This kind of economy of working has persisted. The metal is no longer valuable, but smiths still habitually save odd pieces in the scrap pile, to provide the material for a particular job or special tool. There is a powerful appeal in having an excuse to forage in scrapyards for handy bits, and if you can't exactly forge a sword into a ploughshare, you might at least make a candleholder out of an old piece of pipe.

The intrinsic self-sufficiency of smithing is of great benefit to the amateur and professional alike. You can begin with very little equipment and make what you need as time goes by.

Blacksmithing offers a way of working metal that gives rise to forms and qualities that are far more personal than the products of our machine-made environment. There is a freedom and spontaneity in shaping hot metal with a hammer. Every blow leaves its mark and contributes to the result. Each smith will hit the metal in his own way and leave a characteristic 'fingerprint' of hammer marks. You don't have to search for this, it will come to you.

So what kind of objects do blacksmiths make today? The answer is an almost embarrassingly long list, from small items such as hooks, paperknives and candleholders through light fittings, curtain rails and furniture, to pieces of architectural metalwork such as screens, railings and gates and large pieces of public art. The point is, the choice is yours. The craft encompasses all these things but the processes used to make them are essentially the same.

This book looks at processes as the basic building blocks through which you can realize and develop your own projects and ideas. The challenge, the fun – and indeed the magic – lies in playing with fire and transforming a rather unprepossessing material into something with a quality and life of its own.

Finally, the techniques and processes that I describe are those that from my experience have proved to be the most effective. They are not necessarily *the* way these things should be done. When I started smithing I learnt a great deal by spending a day a week in a well-established forge that employed a number of blacksmiths. I had a forge to myself, would spend half a day struggling to do something until someone took pity and showed me how to do it. Problem solved. Until later another smith would wander over and say 'If I were you I wouldn't do it like that – what I would do is this....'. It was the best lesson of all. In the end there is no definitive way, only the way that works for you.

Sculptural piece by Alan Evans, gas cut from steel tube, heated and shaped.

1 WORKSHOP AND EQUIPMENT

THE WORKSPACE

Setting up your own workshop is a crucial step and there are a number of important points to be taken into account when considering the use of a particular building or space. The essential requirements are size, accessibility and an electric power supply.

To begin blacksmithing the nature of the space is more important than the size. My first workshop was only 2.4m (8ft) long by 2m (6ft 3in) wide, but it did have the virtue of a concrete floor and a high ceiling. If there is room for a forge and anvil, and enough space to move comfortably around the anvil, you have a potential forging workshop; minimal but viable. This said, a bigger space is clearly desirable, allowing more equipment to be fitted and space to lay out and construct larger projects. But if a small space is all you have, do not be discouraged.

A concrete floor is very desirable but not as essential as a ceiling high enough to allow you to swing a hammer at full stretch – 2.4m (8ft) is a minimum. Do not forget that light fittings are usually lower than the ceiling itself. It is remarkably easy to remove lights with a careless swing of a hammer, even when you thought you knew where they were. Ceiling lights should be placed high up and out of reach. A large workspace is no good if the roof is too low.

Access is a major consideration. Moving equipment, metal, fuel and so on into the building requires a reasonably easy access. Steps, for example, are a real problem. A level access and a wide door – preferably double doors – are a great advantage. It is so easy to put together a large piece of work, and forget that it has to be taken out of the workshop when it is finished.

Fire risk must also be evaluated. The most suitable type of building is of conventional brick, concrete or stone construction with slate or tile roofing, or utilitarian steel framing and metal cladding. Whilst this does not preclude the use of a wooden shed, it does mean that more care must be exercised than in, say, a brick building. This may mean lining a special part of the workshop with non-inflammable sheeting for welding or grinding. A wooden shed also needs a hard, preferably concrete, floor.

OPPOSITE PAGE: Tool rack for hammers, fullers, hot chisels and punches.

The author's first workshop. Just enough room for a coke forge, anvil and vices fitted to a bench.

It must be acknowledged that noise is a potential problem. In my experience, not quite so much the noise of hammering at an anvil, but the whining noise of ancillary equipment such as a fan or angle grinder. Clearly if your intended forging shop is adjacent to the house next door, you may have a problem. Distance can make a difference and a screen of shrubs and trees may help. Working only at particular times of the day – never after 6pm, for example – might also help endear you to your neighbours.

ELECTRIC POWER AND LIGHTING

Electric power is essential. Even if you wish to blow your forge with traditional bellows, you will still need to have electric light to see what you are doing. If your workshop is situated where you live, a catenary wire run from the house carrying the power cable is not difficult to arrange. The power should come through its own fuse in your domestic consumer unit. Fit a fuse rather than a miniature circuit breaker, if you are going to use an arc welder. This will tend to trip the circuit breaker, while a wire fuse is more tolerant.

It is better to fit more power sockets than you think you need, and preferably use double ones to reduce the hazard of long trailing leads to a hand electric drill or angle grinder. With so much metal in the workshop, good earthing is essential. RCD (Residual Current Device) sockets are also a worthwhile safety device, giving you protection should you cut a trailing cable with a power tool or a piece of hot metal.

Traditionally a blacksmith's workshop was an ill-lit place, with few windows, since the smith needed to 'see the colour of the metal'. That is, to judge its temperature. It is very important to be able to see how hot the metal is, but this does not mean that the workshop has to be gloomy. A normally lit interior space allows you to judge the colour of the metal perfectly well, and crucially enables you to see what you are doing. A light-coloured floor and walls provide a good background against which you can judge a bar for straightness. If the floor and walls are a dark colour, it may be necessary to use a piece of white painted board propped up, to act as a background.

Direct sunlight can be a problem. For this reason, windows may be better fitted with obscured glass and ideally should be in a north-facing wall. Sunlight coming directly through a window and shining on the metal, can make judging the heat very difficult. If there is really no alternative – or if you want to work out of doors for instance – the hot end of the metal can be offered into a steel drum, or under the shade of the forge hood, where its colour can be seen.

For preference, windows should be set fairly high. If they are at bench height or lower, they can be easily broken by the careless handling of a length of metal or a dropped tool. A window above a bench is a good arrangement from the point of view of illumination, but beware of grinding sparks impacting the glass. The metal particles stick and gradually turn the window brown with rust.

A good flat, solid floor is important, not least because blacksmithing equipment is heavy and subject to impact. A smooth

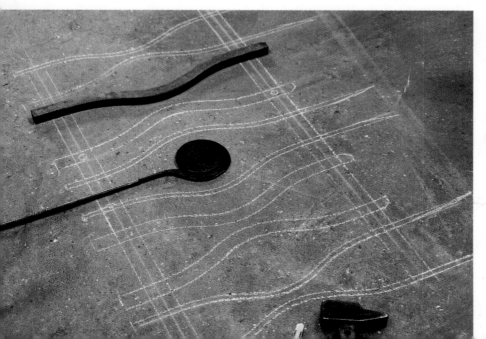

A fence design laid out on the concrete workshop floor.

concrete floor is fireproof, enables equipment to be moved easily and allows chalk lines to be set out as a guide for a particular piece of work. If the floor is truly level as well as flat, a spirit level can be used to check pieces of work and a plumb line hung from the roof will be at right angles to the floor surface. This can be very useful for ensuring that an upright feature – the stem of a floor standing lamp, for instance – is set truly vertical in relation to its base.

The workshop should be well ventilated, but not draughty. There is a risk of fumes from the forge fire and from arc welding operations. A coal or coke fire is dusty, and grinding produces dust. For these reasons, many smiths prefer to work with the door open to provide a flow of fresh air. But a direct draught near the fire should be avoided since it can blow fumes from the burning fuel into the workshop before they can escape up the flue.

BASIC EQUIPMENT AND LAYOUT

Essential equipment is the forge, anvil, a heavy vice and a bench. A great deal can be achieved with just these and a few hand tools. It is an advantage to add a hand electric angle grinder, an electric arc welder, and a number of other tools that will be reviewed in Chapter 15. But whatever else you may have, or aspire to, the forge and anvil are the heart of the workshop.

The forge is simply a heat source and may be coal, coke, gas or oil-fired. There are many different types and sizes, each with its own advantages and disadvantages (*see* box pages 12–13). Like motor cars, they all ultimately get you there, but with varying degrees of efficiency, comfort, speed and cost.

Since it needs a flue, a coal or coke forge tends to fix the layout of the workshop. Its position needs careful thought. A gas-fired forge running on propane, or an oil-fired

forge burning paraffin needs no flue in a well-ventilated workshop, since the fuel burns cleanly without noxious fumes. It should be remembered, however, that any kind of hydrocarbon fuel produces carbon dioxide, and with a restricted air supply can also produce carbon monoxide. So good ventilation is important. These forges provide a heated chamber – similar to a potters kiln – accessed though doors at front and back. Since they are relatively light in construction, and do not need a fixed flue, they can be placed on a base fitted with castors, and moved as necessary. This permits a more flexible layout to the workshop, enabling the forge to be sited to suit the particular job.

Solid fuel forges often have a water trough attached to the front of the hearth. It is essential to have some form of tank or trough in which to cool or quench the metal. An old oil drum may serve, although there is some advantage in having a long tank, since a hot bar may be laid across it and areas quenched at either side of a heat, without flooding too much water on the floor.

WORKSHOP LAYOUT

Positioning the forge fire is probably the most crucial decision to make in planning the layout of the workshop. If you are only expecting to work short pieces of metal, the location of the forge may not seem to be critical. But consider the need to heat one end of a long length of metal, to make (for example) a 2m curtain rail or a long crowbar. Will the other end hit the wall? Or the need may arise to heat the middle of a long length, to bend it. The space at either side of the forge will determine the maximum length that can be handled. Anticipating the worst case enables the forge to be placed in a position that permits maximum use.

It is well worth drawing a plan of the workshop, and taking time to determine

WHICH FORGE?

COAL OR COKE FORGES

Advantages

◆ Give a short heat on a bar.
◆ Good for providing a local heat in the middle of a bar, to make a tight bend for example.
◆ Very suitable for fire-welding operations.
◆ Flexible access to the heat source – a large or awkward piece may be reheated.
◆ Since a fan controls the fire, it may be shut down between heats, conserving fuel.
◆ If the fan is silenced, it can be very quiet to use.

Disadvantages

◆ More difficult to install. Must have a flue to vent fumes.
◆ Dirty. Even with a good flue it produces dust in the workshop.
◆ Difficult to achieve a heat much longer than, perhaps, 6in (15cm).
◆ Metal left unattended in the fire will almost certainly burn.
◆ Physically a larger unit than a gas or oil forge.

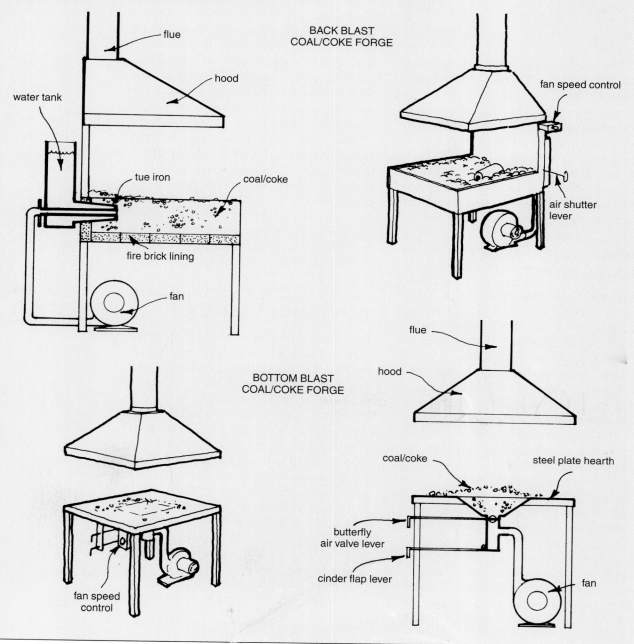

WHICH FORGE?

GAS OR OIL FORGES

Advantages

◆ Easy to install – no flue.

◆ Can be made mobile by placing on a trolley fitted with castors.

◆ Give a long heat on a bar – as long as the forge chamber itself – good for long tapers or long bends.

◆ Several bars may be heated at once and worked in rotation. Ideal for repetition forging.

◆ Metal left in the fire will not burn, though the surface may oxidize considerably.

◆ Physically a smaller unit than a solid-fuel forge.

Disadvantages

◆ Not very suitable for taking short heats on a bar.

◆ Local heat in the middle of a bar is determined by the length of the chamber.

◆ Limited access. Once a bar is bent, it may not be possible to get it back into the forge.

◆ Demands intensive use. Once lit, expensive fuel burns continuously.

◆ It may be difficult to achieve fire welding temperatures.

◆ Even with a silenced fan, the roar of the flame can be noisy.

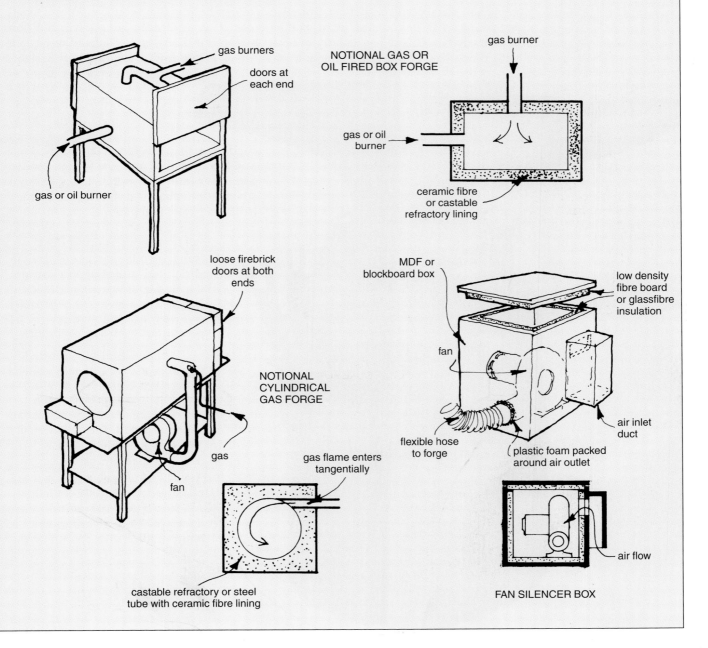

gas burners

doors at each end

gas or oil burner

NOTIONAL GAS OR OIL FIRED BOX FORGE

gas burner

gas or oil burner

ceramic fibre or castable refractory lining

loose firebrick doors at both ends

NOTIONAL CYLINDRICAL GAS FORGE

gas

fan

gas flame enters tangentially

castable refractory or steel tube with ceramic fibre lining

MDF or blockboard box

low density fibre board or glassfibre insulation

fan

flexible hose to forge

plastic foam packed around air outlet

air inlet duct

air flow

FAN SILENCER BOX

the optimum position for the forge. Cutting a hole though the roof to put in a flue is something you really only want to do once. The rest of the workshop can then be laid out around the forge. Take advantage of the access door. It may be possible, for example, to feed long lengths of metal through the door into a vice or mechanical saw, to cut them off.

The anvil should normally be close to the forge. There is a great advantage in being able to take a piece of metal from the fire to the anvil, in one movement, before it cools down. This is particularly critical with thin stock. A vice – preferably a leg vice – should also be positioned where hot metal from the fire can be quickly clamped and worked with the minimum of running around. Safety, comfort and efficiency are worth striving for and after a little time in the workshop you may be able to refine the layout to your advantage.

ANVILS

When choosing an anvil, it is worth remembering that you can make small pieces of work on a large anvil, but you can't easily make large pieces of work on a small anvil. Anvils are rated by weight, which is the important factor in absorbing the shock of hammering. Since volume determines weight, a 200lb (90kg) anvil may only be a few inches longer than a 100lb (45kg) anvil, So, if you have a choice (and the space), choose the larger one. This principle applies to a lot of tools including a vice, leg vice, bench drill, fly press, lathe and so on. An anvil weighing less than 1cwt (50kg) is likely to be too small for much serious work.

There are two basic types of anvil in common use, the London pattern and the double bick anvil, widely used in Europe, a version of which is called the Portsmouth pattern in Britain. New anvils are available and used ones may be bought from engineering machinery dealers, farm auctions or even scrapyards. Some may actually *be* scrap, but few anvils are totally beyond salvaging.

Anvils today are made of a steel casting with the face hardened, but traditionally were made with a wrought iron or soft steel body and a separate hardened steel face, fire-welded on. Many anvils had the steel plate welded to leave part of the body exposed as a step or table of soft iron, that provides a surface used for cutting, since it will not blunt a chisel. Exceptionally the plate may be in the process of separating from the body of the anvil. A 'cracked' or

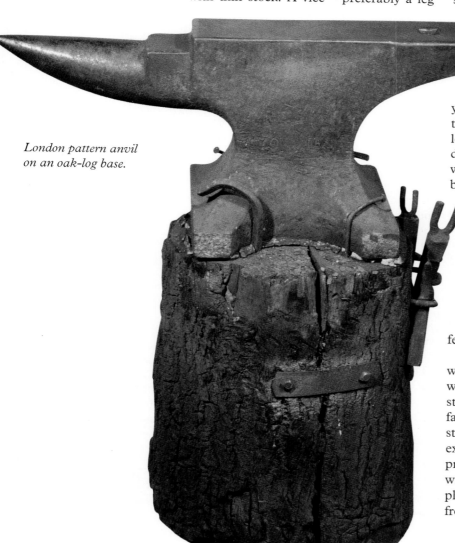

London pattern anvil on an oak-log base.

'dull' note when tapping along the anvil with a hammer may indicate this problem.

Much is made in the literature of choosing an anvil with 'a good clear ring', which is intended to diagnose this kind of fault, in the way that a railway man walks the length of a train, tapping the wheels with a long hammer to check for cracks. In use, however, the last thing you need is an anvil ringing like a bell every time you hit it. A 'good clear ring' can be deafening. Setting the anvil on timber and bedding the feet of the anvil on a few strips of modelling clay (plasticine), will deaden and control the ring (*see* box pages 16–17).

WORKBENCH

The bench provides a focus for the cold work needed to deal with the pieces you have forged. It is a place where you can fix a vice, check, clean up, file, fit, assemble, and simply put down components while you consider the next step. It may be large or small, depending on the space available and kind of work you want to do, and made of timber or metal. A metal bench (or at least a metal top to a bench) may be useful if it is to double as a bench for gas or arc welding. Either way, make it rigid and err on the side of heaviness. A shelf under the bench top is doubly useful since it provides storage and adds weight to the structure.

An engineer's vice or a leg vice (or both) should be fixed to the bench in a position where they offer the best access. It is useful to have an engineer's vice with a swivel base fitted at one corner of the bench, enabling it to be swung round to provide access both from the side and the end of the bench. Flexibility is useful in this instance and as a general principle. You never know the shape, size and length of metal you are going to need to work next, and it is an irritating problem if part of it fouls the wall or the leg of a bench.

Part of the bench top can provide a good clear layout area. You may also want to

have a surface plate on the bench to provide a flat reference surface for checking or assembling components. This does not need to be of the precision ground quality used in an engineering workshop, but simply a piece of flat steel plate, carefully checked for straightness with a steel rule, or a salvaged cast-iron machine table from a scrapyard. It can be an advantage to set this up using a spirit level so that it is truly level.

VICES

There are two types of vice commonly used in a blacksmith's shop, a leg vice and a bench or engineer's vice. They operate on different principles. The engineer's vice has jaws that remain parallel at any opening, while the jaws of the leg vice pivot on an arc. It is useful to have both, but if space or cost is a limitation, the first choice should be a leg vice. This can be fitted to a bench, can be obtained already fitted to a free-standing

Double bick anvil on an angle-iron base.

WHICH ANVIL?

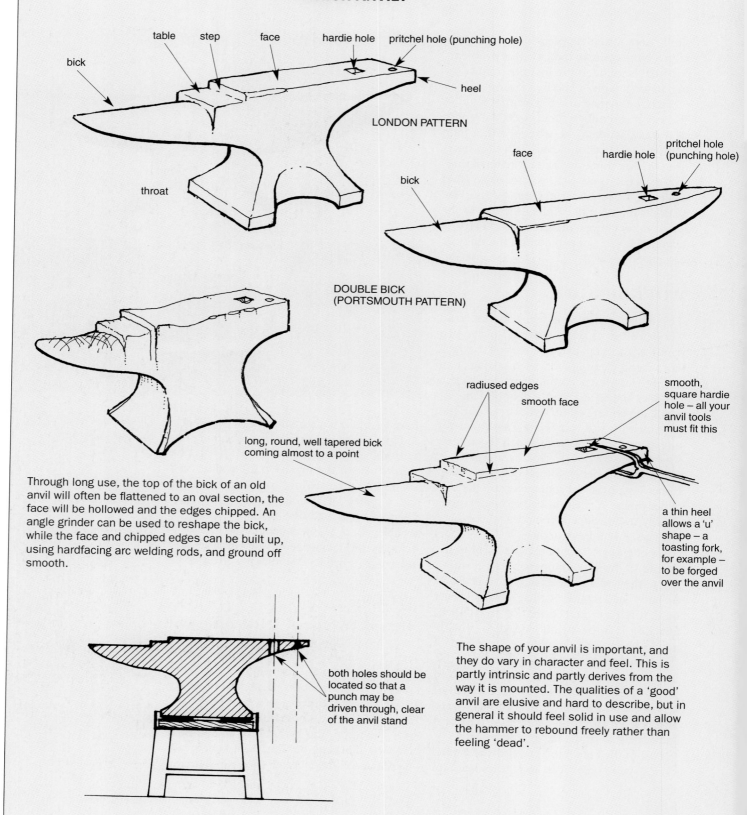

LONDON PATTERN

bick · table · step · face · hardie hole · pritchel hole (punching hole) · heel · throat

face · hardie hole · pritchel hole (punching hole) · bick

DOUBLE BICK (PORTSMOUTH PATTERN)

long, round, well tapered bick coming almost to a point

radiused edges

smooth face

smooth, square hardie hole – all your anvil tools must fit this

a thin heel allows a 'u' shape – a toasting fork, for example – to be forged over the anvil

Through long use, the top of the bick of an old anvil will often be flattened to an oval section, the face will be hollowed and the edges chipped. An angle grinder can be used to reshape the bick, while the face and chipped edges can be built up, using hardfacing arc welding rods, and ground off smooth.

both holes should be located so that a punch may be driven through, clear of the anvil stand

The shape of your anvil is important, and they do vary in character and feel. This is partly intrinsic and partly derives from the way it is mounted. The qualities of a 'good' anvil are elusive and hard to describe, but in general it should feel solid in use and allow the hammer to rebound freely rather than feeling 'dead'.

WHICH ANVIL?

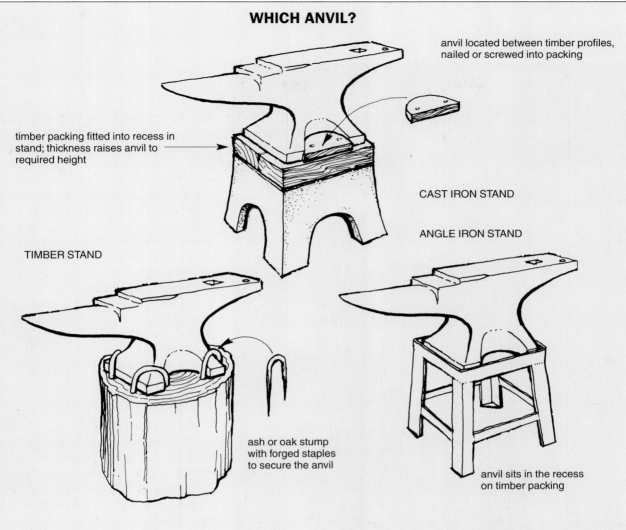

anvil located between timber profiles, nailed or screwed into packing

timber packing fitted into recess in stand; thickness raises anvil to required height

CAST IRON STAND

ANGLE IRON STAND

TIMBER STAND

ash or oak stump with forged staples to secure the anvil

anvil sits in the recess on timber packing

MOUNTING THE ANVIL

The height of the anvil is a matter of personal taste, but in general it should be set so that when you stand comfortably with a relaxed arm, a bar held in the hand lies horizontally on the anvil face. The traditional test is to stand upright beside the anvil with an arm hanging down. If the knuckles of a gently closed fist just touch the anvil face, then it is at your working height.

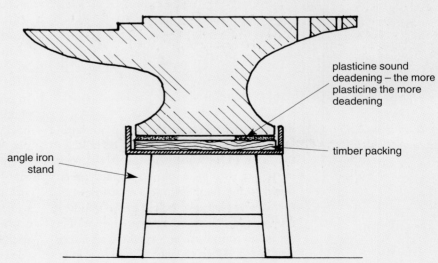

plasticine sound deadening – the more plasticine the more deadening

timber packing

angle iron stand

TYPICAL SOUND DEADENING

Leg vice on a mounting bolted to the floor.

example – it may be subject to as much impact as an anvil.

As with anvils, new leg vices are available, but serviceable old ones are to be had from similar sources. It is fairly easy to check that the clamping screw is not damaged, the jaws meet properly and the bottom pivot is not out of line or loose. The jaws of a leg vice are integral with the body and are sometimes not hardened, but may be patterned to give a grip surface. This grip should be ground off to leave smooth jaws, or they will make marks on a hot workpiece.

The bench vice usually does have hardened jaw faces with a grip patterned surface. These are separate pieces retained with screws, and are better removed and replaced with smooth mild steel jaws, to avoid marking workpieces. It is useful to have a vice fitted with a swivel base.

STANDS

If you work alone, you are very likely to find occasions when it would be helpful to have another hand. Simply hot cutting the end off a long or heavy bar can become a real problem, without someone to hold it for you. An adjustable stand with a tripod base offers a way of supporting the other end of the bar and solving the problem. This is sometimes referred to as a 'blacksmith's helper'. It is useful to have several of these. Different supporting pieces can be made to fit to the basic stand, some with plain ends, some with a flat 'u' shape to prevent the bar falling off sideways, and some with a roller to allow a bar to be slid backwards and forwards when, for example, splitting it down its length.

Quite different kinds of stand – trestles – may be needed if you are intending to make any kind of gate, grille or screen. These usually have simple 'A' frame ends and an angle iron or flat bar horizontal. They are used in pairs (or more) and are carefully levelled to provide a reliable horizontal surface on which the structure may be assembled.

mounting, or you can make a mounting from heavy tube or 'I' beam to be bolted to the floor. However it is installed, the virtue of the leg is to transmit the impact directly down to the floor. Fitting a vice to a stand that can be placed or bolted in the middle of the floor can be an advantage, since it offers access all round. Again, weight is an important factor. When the vice is used to grip hot metal – to be hammered into a bend for

SWAGE BLOCK

This is not the most essential item when you are starting a workshop, but is nevertheless a very useful and versatile piece of equipment. A swage block is usually square in shape, made of cast iron, has a number of square, round and rectangular holes passing through it, and grooves of different profiles cast into its edges. Some have a cavity for shaping the bowl of a ladle. The block can be used on the floor, but is better set on a stand which enables it to be laid flat or stood on edge.

With the block laid flat, the holes serve variously as heading tools, to anchor the end of a bar for bending, provide sockets for

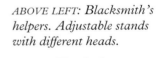

ABOVE LEFT: Blacksmith's helpers. Adjustable stands with different heads.

ABOVE: Trestles in use to assemble a grille.

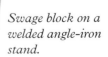

Swage block on a welded angle-iron stand.

tools like swages or fullers and offer support for a hot bar when drifting through large holes. On edge, the block can serve as a collection of bottom swages of larger sizes than anvil swages, it can locate a bar horizontally, and bars can be hammered straight or bent into curves across the larger hollow profiles. Again, the heavier the block the better.

HAND TOOLS

Working hot metal can ultimately demand a large number of tools, not least because while the metal is workable, you cannot touch it. But you can begin smithing with a relatively small number, and as your skills develop, make many of the more specialized tools yourself.

Blacksmithing tools are produced commercially, or you can save money by seeking second-hand tools at machinery dealers, scrapyards, farm sales, car boot sales and junk shops. Work with just a few tools initially. With a little experience you will be in a far better position to select the tools that suit both you and the kind of work you want to do.

The shiny painted and varnished hammer handle, for instance, is the last thing you really need to hold for three hours in a sweaty hand. Plain, unvarnished hickory or ash handles are preferable, even if you have to spend time scrubbing off the varnish with steel wool. Similarly avoid plastic or rubber-sheathed handles on any tools used near hot metal. Even the plastic case of a tape measure is at risk.

Hammers

You probably only need one or two hammers to begin with, but you may need to try several in order to locate the right ones. I do much of my work with three different hammers and most of it with just one. A weight between 1¾lbs and 3½lbs (roughly 0.75kg to 1.6kg) will be suitable for most forging processes, but occasionally a smaller or larger hand hammer may be needed. A 7lb or 10lb (3kg or 4.5kg) sledge hammer is also useful, even if you work alone (Hammers may be marked in pounds, ounces, kilograms or grammes). Many smiths use a conventional engineer's pattern, ball-pein hammer, but my preference is for a square-faced, cross-pein hammer, for reasons explained in Chapter 5. This is the common pattern available in Germany and France.

Mallets

A heavy mallet is useful to straighten or bend metal without damaging its surface. A hot bar can be worked on a timber block. Timber, rubber and rawhide-headed mallets are available, although timber is usually too light. The type that has a steel head fitted with replaceable rawhide faces is ideal, and available in several weights. It is also obtainable with one rawhide face and one copper, that can be useful in its own right, and adds weight.

BELOW: My favourite forging hammers, two square-faced cross-pein hammers and a ball pein.

RIGHT: Two rawhide mallets and one with a heavy rubber head.

Tongs

The jaws of blacksmith's tongs are shaped to fit a particular section of bar – round, square, flat – and may also only accept one particular size. Most tongs are designed to hold a workpiece securely while it is hammered, but some are intended for picking up metal from the fire, bending small details or for opening and setting collars. Choose tongs that suit the work you want to do. Many tongs seem to be made far too long and heavy. Small light tongs are preferable unless you are undertaking very large and heavy work. The jaws can be adjusted, so two or three pairs may serve initially for a wide variety of work. It can be useful to make a few oval rings from steel rod to slip over the handles of the tongs to lock a workpiece in the jaws.

ANVIL TOOLS

The hardie hole in the anvil accepts a variety of tools. The most essential and often used is the hardie itself, used for cutting off metal. Hardies can be short and squat for cutting cold metal or more slender in shape for hot cutting. It can be useful to have two hot hardies, one forged and

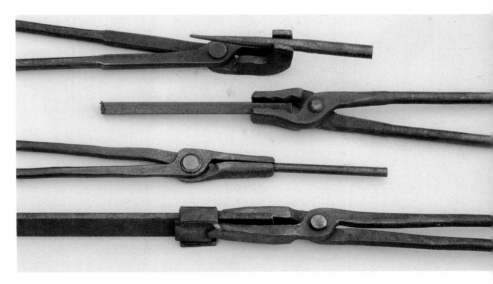

Tongs for holding particular bar sections.

sharpened symmetrically, the other forged with a vertical face and ground on one side only, like a wood chisel.

When buying anvil tools make sure that the shank size fits your anvil. Even if nominally correct, the shanks may need to be ground slightly to provide a snug fit.

LEFT: *A hardie in use for hot cutting.*

ABOVE: *Bottom fullers.*

Fullers and swages

Fullers are of a convex shape, swages are concave. Both are often used in pairs as 'top and bottom tools'. Bottom tools have a square steel shank that fits the hardie hole. Top tools have an iron or steel rod handle wrapped round the body, or a wooden handle fitted into an eye like a hammer. In my

Bottom swages.

BELOW: *Top fullers, two with timber handles and one with a rodded handle.*

BOTTOM: *Top swages, two with timber handles and one with a rodded handle.*

view, the wooden shafted tools are easier to use. They are often lighter, usually better balanced and more comfortable to hold.

Chisels

Chisels for hot cutting, similarly fitted with rod or timber handles, are known as 'hot sets'. 'Set tools' are, in general, those fitted with a separate handle, rather than held directly in the hand. They are held in position on the work and hit with a hammer – often a sledgehammer. There are set punches and set hammers, a useful version of which is known as a 'flatter', used for smoothing and flattening surfaces. In each case, the handle keeps the smith's hand away from the heat of the metal and the risk of a misplaced hammer blow. Many of these tools can be used by a smith working alone, but in reality they belong to a category of tools intended to be used when working with a striker – the helper with the sledgehammer. The smith holds the workpiece and places the set tool, while the striker provides the blow.

There are also hand-held versions of these tools. Chisels, punches, fullers and more rarely swages can be tools directly held in the hand, and struck with a hand

ABOVE: *Hot sets. Chisels for cutting hot metal.*

ABOVE: A flatter (left) and a set hammer (right).

Hand chisels; (top) curved chisels; (bottom) straight chisels, some converted from builder's star drills.

hammer. Some people find it easier to use hand chisels and punches initially, because although they require a little confidence to use, they demand that you stand closely over the work in a position where you can place the tool more accurately and see its effect more clearly. Set tools allow you to stand further back and for this reason beginners may have difficulty in, for example, placing a chisel or punch on the centre line of a bar.

Wire Brushes

It is useful to have a wire brush constantly available while working at the anvil. Forge scale builds up on the hot metal and in a coal or coke fire, small pieces of molten clinker will stick to the workpiece. Left in place, continued forging pounds clinker and scale into the metal and when this is eventually removed, a rough pitted surface will remain. Scale is less adhesive at high temperatures, so a vigorous brushing while the metal is at yellow heat is the most effective way of cleaning the surface. It is good practice to brush the workpiece every so often to remove debris.

Wire brushes are widely available in tool and hardware shops. These consist of round spring wire tufts set in a wooden handle (not plastic), the more dense the tufts, the better. There is another type of wire brush called a 'butcher's block brush', that uses flat spring steel wire, set in a substantial wooden handle. These are used by butchers to clean the large timber blocks on which they cut meat, and are available from Butchers' Suppliers. These brushes are harder to find, but offer a more aggressive action and last longer.

GENERAL PURPOSE TOOLS

General purpose tools are needed by the smith, just as they are needed by other metalworkers. In some cases special versions of standard tools are also used by the blacksmith. General purpose tools can be categorized as follows.

Measuring Tools

These include steel rule, steel tape measure, callipers, and engineer's squares. Folding 2ft rules made in brass were the traditional blacksmith's version, since unlike plain steel rules, they did not rust in the workshop. But stainless-steel or satin chrome-plated rules are readily available today and are clearer to read. Special blacksmithing callipers with a long handle are useful for gauging the sizes of hot metal, since they keep your hand away from the heat. A small square is useful for checking, for example, that the end of a bar is cut square, while a large square – 2ft long – is needed to check the frame of a gate.

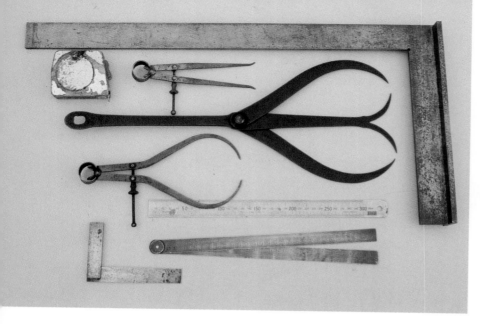

Measuring tools; (top to bottom) large engineer's square, steel tape measure, spring inside callipers, blacksmith's double callipers, spring outside callipers, satin chrome steel rule, brass folding rule, small engineer's square.

Marking tools; centre punches, dividers, scriber, French chalk.

Marking Tools

These include scriber, dividers, French chalk and centre punch. A scriber is used against a square or steel rule to scratch a line in cold metal to mark a cutting edge, or set out the positions of holes. Dividers provide a means of scribing circles or arcs and are also useful for dividing a given length into an equal number of parts. French chalk can be used to mark metal hot or cold. It can be sharpened to a more durable point than blackboard chalk and can tolerate and remain visible on metal that is at dull red heat. Blackboard chalk spits off hot metal and disappears at a relatively low temperature.

Centre punches are used to mark the positions of holes prior to drilling or punching. A small engineer's centre punch is useful for marking cold metal, while a larger punch is useful for making a deep impression, more readily seen when the metal is hot. The spring-operated type that makes a mark when pressed down, is particularly useful for marking through an existing hole to locate another, without the need for three hands.

Cutting Tools

These should include hacksaws and files, and ideally a hand electric angle grinder. A hacksaw frame for 10in and 12in blades may initially be all you have to cut off metal, so it is worth buying a good sturdy one that allows the blade to be adjusted to a range of angles. High Speed Steel (HSS) blades or 'bi-metal' blades, that have high-speed steel teeth welded to a softer steel body, are preferable for cutting mild steel. Carbon-steel blades may be temptingly cheap, but will blunt almost immediately, and are really only worth buying to cut non-ferrous metals.

Files can be useful for removing burrs and sharp edges, easing out a hole or smoothing a surface. In general they are intended for working cold metal, but coarse files – rasps – may be used with more rapid effect to shape hot metal. Caution should be exercised in cold-filing visible parts of a forged component since the black forged surface will be cut through, leaving bright scratch marks. Reheating the metal to red heat will, however, oxidize the surface and disguise the filing

A hand electric angle grinder is a very versatile tool offering a variety of different functions. With a cutting disc fitted, it is quicker than a hacksaw for cutting pieces of metal from a stock length. (And if need be, it can cut hardened steel that would be too hard to cut with a hacksaw blade). It can be fitted with grinding discs for shaping metal or dressing off welds, flexible abrasive discs for refining and polishing metal surfaces, and wire brushes for removing rust or burnishing forged metal. As with a file, the effect of a grinding or flexible abrasive disc can be to destroy the quality of a forged surface. So this function should be used with some care. But if the surface finish left by the grinder is fine enough, reheating the component to red heat will oxidize its surface and restore the appearance. A 100mm (4in) or 115mm (4½in) diameter grinder is all that is needed initially.

STORAGE RACKS

As far as possible all tools should have a place in a rack where they can be stored ready to hand and give you no excuse for leaving them lying about, to be mislaid or become a hazard underfoot. It is preferable to store tools visibly in some kind of wall rack, rather than in drawers where they are hard to find. Many tools will fit easily between two parallel pieces of timber or metal fitted along the wall. Some can simply be hung from long nails or screws driven into the wall, while hand electric tools can be stored in open cupboards.

A rack is also needed for storing steel bar stock. In general it is safer to store bars horizontally, supporting them at intervals to prevent sagging. It is a distinct advantage to be able to see the end of the bar

rack to enable particular sections to be identified. Do not underestimate the dead weight of an accumulation of metal bars. The rack should err on the side of being too sturdy, rather than too light. If space is limited, standard 6m bars can be cut down and stood on end, but care should be taken to prevent them slipping.

Angle grinders, fitted with different discs. (Clockwise from top left) cutting disc, grinding disc, wire brush and paper disc.

Hand electric tools stored in an open cupboard.

2 MATERIALS

Despite (or perhaps because of) hundreds of years of craft and engineering development, metalworking terminology is often ambiguous and confusing. This applies not least to materials themselves. The metallurgy of iron and steel is well described in other books, but a few notes are relevant here.

Metals are not normally commercially available as pure elements. They are all alloys, which is to say a mixture of metals, or of metals and non-metallic elements. Steel is an alloy of iron and carbon. Iron is the pure metal. Particular alloys have been carefully formulated over many years to provide a range of materials, with particular qualities of strength, surface hardness, resistance to corrosion and so on. Similarly they have been tailored to suit particular manufacturing processes such as, machining, cold bending and hot forging.

Although blacksmiths usually forge iron and steel, many other metals can be hot forged, including aluminium, brass, bronze, copper and titanium. However, in each case the appropriate hot forging alloy should be used, or working the metal may prove difficult or impossible. The supplier should be able to identify the correct grade.

'Pure' Iron, or 'butter' iron is now manufactured in Europe as a special, very low carbon iron alloy, that contains as little as 0.002 per cent carbon, 0.08 per cent manganese and traces of other elements. It is more malleable than mild steel, but is considerably more expensive.

Wrought Iron was the traditional material used by the blacksmith. 'wrought' meaning 'worked'. Since the late eighteenth century, wrought iron was produced, using pig iron from a blast furnace – an alloy of iron with perhaps 4 per cent carbon. This was melted in batches in a puddling furnace, where the action of air and iron oxide had the effect of removing almost all the carbon and other impurities, converting much of them into a liquid slag. The resulting mass of pasty metal was forged – wrought – under a power hammer, and rolled to physically consolidate the metal and squeeze out the slag.

Further reheating and reworking was necessary to refine the metal to a good quality; the more reprocessing cycles, the more refined the end product. The result is iron alloyed with a trace amount – maybe 0.05 per cent – carbon, but physically combined with 2–3 per cent silicate slag. This is distributed throughout the metal, giving it a characteristic fibrous structure, similar to the grain in wood, that is produced by the rolling process.

The metal is ideally suited to hot forging – it is malleable and ductile, can be worked at a much higher temperature than mild steel and is readily fire-welded. It is also claimed that wrought iron does not corrode so easily as mild steel. But being produced by a hand-controlled process, wrought iron is variable in quality and, like timber, it can split or crack along the grain. Care is therefore needed in selecting material suitable for a particular piece of work. Wrought iron ceased large-scale commercial production a generation ago, but is still available as re-rolled bar and plate in a limited range of sizes, but is more expensive than mild steel.

OPPOSITE PAGE: Detail of mild steel table top, textured in the fire.

Steels are alloys of iron and carbon, often with additions of other elements. In general, the higher the carbon content, the stronger the steel and the greater its hardness when heat treated. A very important characteristic of steels is their ability to be hardened when rapidly chilled from red heat. The degree to which hardening takes place depends on the carbon content. After chilling or 'quenching', the steel may be so hard that it is too brittle for use, so the hardness is reduced to the desired extent by 'tempering' the metal by reheating to a particular temperature, well below red heat, and allowing it to cool.

Small differences in the amount of carbon in steel can have a dramatic effect on its properties. The steel in a hammer head contains probably 0.75 per cent carbon, only about half of one per cent more than in the mild steel being hammered. As carbon content increases, the steel becomes harder but it also becomes more brittle. So there is a trade-off between hardness and toughness.

Steels much above 1.5 per cent carbon become too brittle to be useful. But at 2.5 per cent carbon content, the alloy changes its name from steel to **cast iron**. This is an alloy of moderate strength, lacking ductility, but is good for casting processes. Cast iron cannot be forged. At red heat it crumbles and tears when hit with a hammer.

Mild steel is the low carbon and iron alloy that replaced wrought iron as a general purpose engineering and structural material. Today, it is the metal most commonly used by blacksmiths. It is indistinguishable in appearance from wrought iron, unless the latter is corroded or etched, showing the grain structure. The carbon content is low enough for heating and quenching to have little effect on the hardness of the metal. It is 'mild' in the sense that it is relatively soft. As **black mild steel** bar, it is specified in Britain by British Standard EN 10025:1993. This calls for a carbon content of around 0.2 per cent.

Bearing in mind, for example, that 18-carat gold contains only 75 per cent gold, but is still called 'gold', you might be forgiven for calling mild steel 'iron'. For this reason it is hard to argue that terms like 'ironwork' or 'forging iron' are incorrect. But 'mild steel' is strictly the proper term and serves to distinguish it from wrought iron.

Black mild steel is the cheapest grade of steel commonly available and is so called because of the layer of dark grey oxide (mill scale) left on the surface after the section has been hot rolled to shape in the rolling mill. Round sections may not be truly round, and square or flat sections tend to have a small radius at the corners. 'Bright' mild steel is more expensive but is chemically very similar in specification although it looks quite different. This has been pickled in acid to remove the mill scale, then cold rolled between polished rollers. This gives the finished section a more precise size, imparts a shiny finish to it and work-hardens the metal. Square or flat sections also have sharp corners. Bright mild steel can be hot forged, and becomes indistinguishable from black mild steel.

Black mild steel is available in a range of solid sections, round, square, flat, angle, channel, 'I' beam and so on. It is also available as round, square or rectangular tube. In Britain, sizes are in metric units, but are in many instances essentially a conversion of inch dimensions into millimetres. Thus, for example, 15mm round or square is not available but 16mm (⅝in) is. To avoid damage in transit, thinner sections such as 6mm round rods, are usually stocked in lengths of around 4m (roughly 13ft). Thicker bars, the majority of the material a blacksmith is likely to use, are generally available in a standard length of 6m (roughly 20ft). The larger structural tube, channel, angle and beam sections are available in standard lengths of 7.6m (25ft) and longer.

Carbon steel is, on the face of it, an unnecessary term, since steel is an alloy of iron and carbon. But it tends to be used to distinguish simple steels – essentially alloys containing just iron and carbon – from those that include other elements.

Alloy steels are steels containing other metals such as manganese, nickel, chromium, vanadium, and so on. Many of these enhance the heat treatment capability of the steel, resulting from its carbon content, by enabling thicker sections to be hardened. Other alloy elements provide particular performance or working properties – the ability to maintain strength or retain a cutting edge at high temperatures, for example.

Tool steel is not a precise designation. It is a broad term that covers any kind of hardenable steel from which tools can be made. Many steels could be described as tool steels. Blacksmiths use a variety of steels to make the different tools they need. Some may be bought as specific bar material, some as salvaged vehicle coil springs and torsion bars, road breaker bits or even the spring clips that secure railway lines. Tool steels do not become as soft as mild steel when heated, and are therefore harder to forge.

Stainless steel describes a family of corrosion-resistant steels that contain a minimum of 11 per cent chromium. They usually also contain nickel that improves corrosion resistance and working properties. Forgeable grades of stainless steel bar stock are specified in Britain as grades 304 and 316. The 316 is more corrosion-resistant. These are non-hardenable materials, suitable for structural and decorative applications. Hardenable grades are also available for making cutlery.

Stainless steels are available in an odd variety of different lengths, depending on the stockist and the particular section. Sections may also be in imperial or metric sizes. This needs a little care when ordering or when comparing prices from different suppliers.

Forging stainless steel is hard work, since the hot metal is less malleable than mild steel. Having been worked, the metal is not immediately 'stainless'. Heating, forging, drilling, grinding and even cutting with a hacksaw contaminate the surface of the metal and disrupt the integrity of the passive, chromic oxide film, on which the corrosion resistance depends. Unless this is re-established, rust stains can appear on the metal when the piece is exposed out of doors. Specialist firms exist to pickle stainless steel items of all sizes and leave them with a clean passivated surface, that resists corrosion. They may also be further processed by electropolishing to produce a brighter finish.

Non-ferrous metals are metals and alloys that do not contain iron. It is beyond the scope of this book to offer a great deal of information in this area but it should be noted that blacksmiths are increasingly experimenting with the use of aluminium, copper, brasses, bronzes, titanium and so on. In comparison with mild steel these are all very expensive, which is an inhibiting factor, so they tend to be used as details in a larger mild steel structure, offering a decorative contrast. They are also far less forgiving than mild steel in requiring a much closer control of working temperature.

With the exception of titanium, they all have lower melting points than steel, and need to be forged at substantially lower temperatures. In general, brasses are forged at a very dull red heat; some may need a heat barely visible in daylight. Bronzes and copper can be forged a little hotter. Aluminium has an even lower forging temperature, and shows no heat colour whatever. At a dull red heat it is beginning to melt. The simplest way to judge its temperature is to test it by stroking a splinter of timber across the surface. At a forging heat, the timber will slide and leave a charcoal mark. Titanium, on the other hand, will stand a temperature considerably higher than steel, and can be forged at similar, or somewhat hotter temperatures, than mild steel.

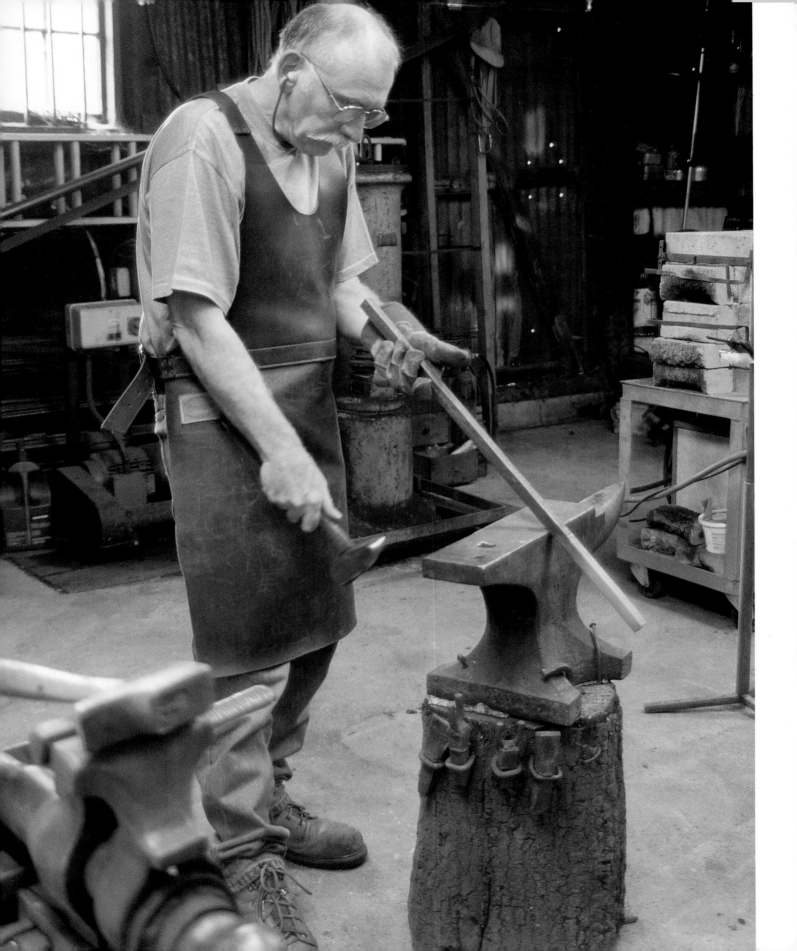

3 HEALTH AND SAFETY

Blacksmithing is a potentially dangerous activity. But so is driving a car, and just as you put on a seat belt and obey the highway code to drive a car, you need to wear protective clothing and develop safe working habits in a blacksmithing workshop. Having taught blacksmithing students in a number of institutions, I have always resisted the idea that 'safety' is an add-on lecture in the curriculum. My conviction is that safety should be an integral part of the way you work. As the old adage has it – the most dangerous thing in the workshop is you. If you are aware of the hazards, you have already gone a long way towards minimizing the risks. In this spirit, safety considerations will be mentioned throughout this book.

Safety is both taking sensible precautions in the way you dress and adopting good working procedures. Working safely should become as instinctive as putting on a seat belt and keeping to the proper side of the white line. And like driving, it is largely common sense.

CLOTHING

Clothes used in the forge need to be robust and comfortable. The general principle is to cover up. The traditional leather blacksmith's apron has a great deal to commend it, and offers a high degree of protection to the front of your body and your legs.

Clothing made from nylon or other synthetic fabrics should be avoided. Sparks can pass straight through a nylon shirt. Or a nylon cuff held too close to a piece of hot metal can melt in an instant. Cotton or wool clothing is preferable. Do not be tempted to wear shorts in the forge in hot weather. It is just too easy for scale or hot metal to fall off the anvil and burn your leg. Cotton jeans, working trousers, or a boiler suit offer worthwhile protection. Wearing a T-shirt with bare arms is about as far as summer clothing goes. Even then, be prepared for the odd piece of forge scale to stick rather painfully to a forearm, before you can brush it off. A long-sleeved shirt will shield your arm from the radiant heat while, for instance, holding a hand chisel over a hot piece of bar.

EYE PROTECTION

The most crucial equipment is eye protection. Current practice favours the use of spectacles with polycarbonate lenses that are highly impact-resistant although they can become scratched. A wide variety of safety spectacles are available, many with cheek protection and side guards. Some may be worn over prescription glasses. The point of wearing safety glasses is not essentially to fend off heavy, flying pieces of metal, but sparks and small particles. A fire – particularly a coke fire – will spit out the occasional hot piece of grit. Forging hot iron or steel produces scale (black iron oxide), particles of which are continually shed as the metal is hit. Since your face is right over the metal as you are forging, it is very easy to a get a piece of scale in your eye.

If you wear prescription spectacles for working at arm's length, they may well offer sufficient protection during ordinary forging. There is an argument for the use of

OPPOSITE PAGE:
Checking a bar for straightness. Note the protective clothing – eye and ear protection, leather apron, glove and safety boots. Note also hardies and anvil forks clipped to the base of the anvil.

RIGHT: Forging with a glove on the left hand.

tinted glasses. These, like sunglasses, filter out heat and ultraviolet radiation which through severe and prolonged exposure can cause eye damage. The lesson is not to stare into the fire. For grinding, enclosed soft plastic goggles are preferable, offering better protection against stray sparks approaching the eye at odd angles. As a matter of habit, put on your safety glasses as soon as you enter the workshop.

GLOVES

It is well worth wearing leather, or leather and cotton work gloves while forging. Many smiths work at the anvil holding the hammer in a bare hand, but wearing a glove on the hand that holds the hot metal. A bare hand has a better grip on the hammer handle. The procedure is always to pick up metal with the gloved hand, never the bare hand. It is very easy to grab a piece of metal that has ceased to show any heat colour, but is still quite hot enough to cause a nasty burn. Treat every piece of metal around the anvil with suspicion, and test it before picking it up by holding a bare palm an inch or two above it, where the heat can be felt. I prefer to use gloves that just cover the wrist. Gauntlets that reach nearly to the elbow are available, but unless you are working very large, hot pieces of metal and need the extra arm protection, I find that the wide flared cuffs tend to funnel in hot forge scale. Trying to shake a hot piece of scale out of a glove is no fun.

FOOTWEAR

Another familiar hazard is dropping something heavy on your foot. Good leather boots that cover the ankle and have steel toe protection are well worth the cost. Leather boots or enclosing shoes, even without steel toecaps, are preferable to open shoes, or trainers with nylon fabric panels. Whatever you wear, the cuffs of your trousers should go over the footwear to prevent hot forge

scale or a hot slug of metal slipping down inside the edge of your boot or shoe. Frantically removing a boot is a memorable experience and demonstrates simultaneously, just how quickly this can be achieved and the inadvisability of wearing nylon socks.

Boots also offer protection against pieces of metal on which you might stub your toe, or sharp spikes and edges waiting to catch you out. Stepping on a scrap of hot metal you have just cut off is a common occurrence. It can melt into the boot sole and stick. Polyurethane soles seem to cope with this better than rubber. The answer is to keep track of the hot fragment and ensure that is out of the way. It is also worth noting that – if you can find them – leather bootlaces are far better than nylon that perversely always seem to be fitted to safety boots but are easily melted by forge scale, grinder sparks or the sparks from gas-cutting.

EAR PROTECTION

Ear defenders that fit over the ear, or plugs that fit into the ear are important if you want to preserve your hearing. I use both types at different times. The noise hazard tends to be sporadic and variable. Using an angle grinder, working at a power hammer and some activities at the anvil clearly create noise of a level and intensity that demands protection. The type of earplugs fitted to a springy plastic frame are very convenient since you can wear them around your neck, where they are always ready for use. The 'earmuff' type can be better when you are working for a sustained period at some noisy activity. At no time should you be experiencing a noise that is actually painful or makes your ears ring. If you do, you should have been wearing protection. But the effect of noise is cumulative and lower levels of noise over a long period can damage hearing.

FORGING TUBE

There has been interest in recent years in forging sections other than just solid bar. Tube can be forged much like solid bar if the wall is reasonably thick. But it does present two safety concerns. With one end in a coal or coke fire, it can funnel unburnt gases out into the workshop (even channel or 'I' beam can do the same). Not only does this present hazards if breathed in, but along with the fumes comes the heat, so the end remote from the fire can become unexpectedly hot. Secondly if the tube is quenched, even at black heat, steam and hot water can shoot out of the end of the tube in dramatic fashion. The answer is to anticipate the problem. Plug the end of the tube with rag, avoid quenching tube if possible but if you do have to, always point it in a safe direction.

GENERAL CONCERNS

Ventilation in the workshop has already been mentioned in the context of forge fumes, but using an angle grinder both to grind or to wire brush a metal surface also fills the workshop with airborne dust. It makes sense to use a mask – even the simple disposable type can make a big difference. Be aware that if you are wire-brushing loose paint on metal salvaged from a scrapyard, it may well contain lead.

Working dangerously is at least as much of a problem as wearing the wrong clothes. The workshop can be a place for experiment and spontaneous activity, but not for thoughtless action. Everything you do should be planned and executed carefully. A disciplined routine is required to work safely in a workshop, involving a multitude of small things, most of which add up to common sense.

Think of other people. Be aware of who or what is behind you as you swing a hammer or manipulate a long length of metal. Learn to anticipate the risks. For example, do not leave materials or tools on the floor, you can trip over them. Have storage places for everything and clear up as you go along. Even short off-cuts of bar can act like tiny rollers under your foot and cause you to slip. Never leave lengths of material, particularly bars you may have forged to a sharp point, clamped with the end projecting from a vice. Never leave long lengths of metal just propped up vertically against the bench or vice. Never hit a file with a hammer, it can shatter, sending splinters everywhere. And so on. None of this is privileged information, it is just the workshop equivalent of not leaving the saucepan handle sticking out from the cooker hob.

Lastly there are two classic accidents that should be mentioned. One is to hit rather wildly at a piece of metal on the anvil, miss it, and have the hammer rebound unexpectedly from the anvil face and hit you on the forehead. The other is to swing round the loose bar handle of a vice to tighten it quickly, only to have it stop suddenly and drop, catching your finger under the knob at the end.

4 WORKING AT THE ANVIL

The core of the blacksmith's activity is working at the anvil. This is not a passive tool like a bench but plays a very active part in the forging process, providing a tool socket, surfaces, holes and edges that contribute as much to the work as the hammer. The right-handed smith generally works with the bick facing to his left, but may need to move to a variety of positions around the anvil to work effectively.

Beginners may not be practised at placing blows with a hammer, but have probably used a hammer at some time to put in nails. Forging requires at least the same degree of accuracy, but the blows are usually heavier. Achieving this involves the whole body, from the hand, arm and upper body, to the position of the legs and feet.

Novice smiths are inclined to hold the hammer too tightly, and use it very rigidly and self-consciously, just as the aspiring young bicycle rider starts by gripping the handlebars until his knuckles go white, stiffly conscious of trying to maintain balance. Once you begin to think less about the act of raising your arm and hammering, and more about the effect of the hammer on the metal, you will begin to relax and your hands, body and feet will find the right position. It becomes as unconscious an activity as riding a bike. And in the same way, the process itself becomes far less important than where you are going or what you are making.

The hammer should be held just tightly enough to control it but allowed to pivot freely in the hand. Beginners tend to stand too far back from the anvil and work, as it were, at arm's length. The shoulder of your hammer hand needs to be almost above the work as you strike. It is important to get in close and work *over* the anvil rather than next to it. A beginner may also only raise the hammer a few inches, tapping, rather than giving a solid blow. Raise the hammer high. The impact is in direct proportion to the height.

Rhythm is important too. Each weight of hammer has its own natural rate of striking. Repeated blows can be struck more quickly with a lighter hammer. This makes a small hammer better, for example, for forging thin material or shaping the head of a rivet. The rhythm of each hammer is soon discovered, if you allow yourself to work with it, rather than against it.

GENERAL PROCEDURES

Some activities require the use of a number of tools in short order, punching and drifting a hole for instance, or simply cutting off metal with a hardie. The hammer should invariably be left ready on the face of the anvil, perhaps with one other tool, but any more tools are likely to become dislodged and fall to the floor. One solution is to use space on the anvil stand, either placing hand tools on its top face, between the feet of the anvil, or fitting staples to the side of the stand to take hardies, bending forks and so on (*see* page 30). Another answer is to make a small table that fits into a tripod stand and can be moved around to provide a place to put tools at anvil level, where they can be quickly reached. This avoids a clutter of tools on the floor, that can trip you up.

Holding a workpiece in tongs is never as easy as simply holding a bar. In consequence it is good practice to forge as much

OPPOSITE PAGE:
Forging at an open-air blacksmithing event. Note that the shoulder is almost over the work.

as you can while the metal is still part of the original bar. Plan the piece (or pieces) so that most of the work is done on the bar, before cutting off and completing the other end in tongs. In this way a component may be forged and cut off the bar on the hardie, leaving the end of the parent bar still hot and needing only a little reheating before forging the next piece. A number of repeat components – tapered pins for example – may be made and cut off, without needing to break the rhythm, or stopping to cool and saw the metal.

As a general principle, work should be planned to conserve the heat, so that the workpiece does not have to be cooled and reheated more than necessary. Depending on the nature of the work, planning the most efficient way of undertaking the job can present an interesting challenge in itself.

It is important to emphasize that even if you are making just one item – say 6in (15cm) long – cut a 'handling length', a convenient piece of metal around 2ft (60cm) long. This should be a comfortable size to hold and of sufficient length that the metal remaining will still be long enough for another job. Longer forged items that need, for example, a foot (30cm) or more of metal, can be made back to back. One end of the bar is worked, then becomes the handle that enables you to forge the other end. It all adds up to an economy of working, not because the metal is expensive but because time is. Since the metal is only forgeable for brief periods while it is hot, there is every incentive to make working time as effective as possible.

There are usually two or three distinct phases to making a forging. The first is to change the section of the bar by tapering, punching, spreading or whatever is needed, but all the time taking care to keep the bar straight. The second is to bend the forged bar to shape. The third may be to assemble this bar with others. This sequence may seem obvious but, unless it is kept in mind, it is remarkably easy to bend a bar too early,

then discover that it is now such a shape that, for example, it is impossible to punch a hole where it is needed.

TAKING A HEAT

The process of heating the workpiece is described as 'taking a heat'. It is a measure of skill for a smith to complete a particular operation 'in one heat'. Linguistically this is also the origin of the phrase 'in the heat of the moment'. Watching a blacksmith, for example, punching and drifting a hole 'in the heat of the moment', brings this expression graphically to life.

Iron and steel have the great virtue of being poor conductors of heat. They have a low thermal conductivity – a measure of the rate at which heat is transferred though the metal. (The thermal conductivity of copper, for example, is nine times greater than that of steel) This property of ferrous metals offers fundamental advantages to the blacksmith. One end of a length of metal can be heated to a yellow heat and will stay hot for a relatively long time, while the other end remains cool, conveniently providing a handle. Eventually, of course, the heat will dissipate through the length of the bar and the cooler end becomes too hot to hold, but this will not happen for several heats.

Crucially, part of a bar may be heated discretely, making it soft and enabling it to be manipulated at a precise position, while the remainder stays cool and rigid. As a poor conductor, the hot metal will stay hot longer because the heat is only slowly transmitted to the rest of the bar. The metal will move the most where it is the hottest. Being able to isolate a heat in this way, gives a level of control to the forging of iron and steel that is far harder to achieve in other metals. In contrast a copper bar will not show a sharp cutoff between a red hot portion and the remaining bar, and the heat will dissipate very rapidly through its length.

To the observer the process of taking a heat, hammering the metal, then returning

it to the fire seems to involve long periods of waiting, punctuated by short bursts of frantic activity. But the heating time is not just a rest. It is very important to maintain concentration and mentally rehearse what you are going to do when the metal is ready. All the necessary tools must be anticipated and placed ready to hand. Unless you work quickly and decisively, the opportunity can be wasted. If you lose focus it is all too easy to plant the hot metal on the anvil only to find that you have left the hammer at the fire. 'Strike while the iron is hot' is not just a figure of speech. Whatever else you may have to do in preparation, it is also crucial to set your mental clock running from the moment the metal goes into the fire, so that you can take it out before it burns.

HEAT COLOURS

Blacksmiths judge the heat of the metal by its 'colour', the glow emitted by the hot bar. It is instructive to heat the end of a piece of mild steel in a good, bright forge fire and take it out when it is as hot as possible. In a coal or coke forge it will reach a yellow-white heat and begin to melt and literally to burn, sparking and sizzling like a firework sparkler. Heating metal to this point – destroying the material – is clearly to be avoided, but just short of this temperature the metal is at its softest and most malleable. Take it from the fire and watch the colour of the metal as it cools. It changes from yellow through orange to red, to a very dull red that can only just be seen in the dark. Finally, although it is still very hot, it emits no glow at all and resumes a black appearance. Observe these colours and become familiar with them.

Many terms have been used to describe heat colours – cherry red, medium cherry, blood red and so on – as a way of identifying particular working temperatures, but these are difficult to define precisely in words, and as such are sometimes more

'Strike while the iron is hot.' Hot cutting.

confusing than helpful. The most crucial heat to recognize is the most effective heat for forging, where the metal is bright yellow and just short of burning.

This temperature, which I shall call 'yellow heat', is used for all the principal forging operations such as tapering, upsetting or punching a hole. At yellow heat the metal is capable of considerable plastic deformation. As it cools to what I shall call 'red heat', it becomes difficult to move plastically but will still bend easily. So while yellow heat is ideal for changing the section of the bar, red heat is better used for bending it to shape. At red heat the hammer is also less likely to leave marks on the bar. So a heat may typically start with heavy blows, taking advantage of a yellow heat to move the metal as much as possible, then finish with lighter blows to bend or straighten the bar.

One other temperature is important – welding heat. This is the bright yellow-white colour as the metal just begins to emit a few sparks. It is, in effect, just beginning to burn. Pulled out of the fire the metal surface looks liquid.

It is important to allow the heat to soak right through the metal. Bearing in mind that steel is a poor conductor, the surface of the metal can show a particular heat colour while the interior is cooler. The thicker the metal, the more likely this is to occur. The answer is a little patience.

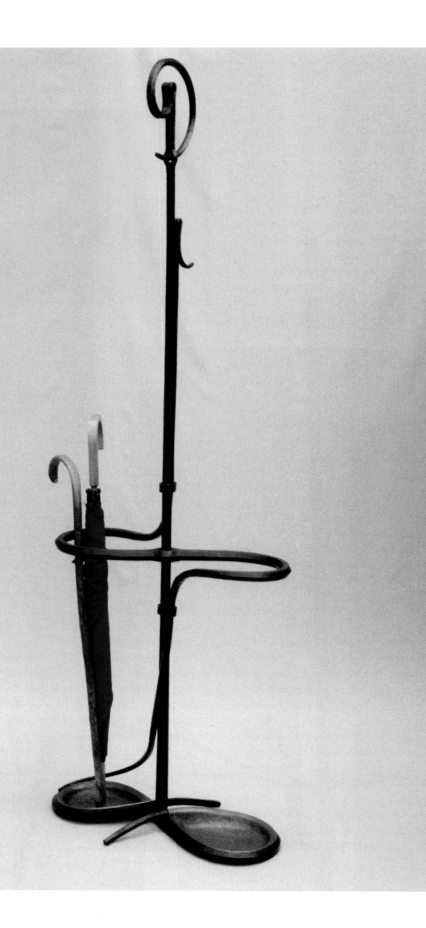

5 DRAWING DOWN

Drawing down involves hammering a bar to reduce its section and increase its length. The classic use is in the taper, an archetypal blacksmithing motif. A taper may be in one plane or in both. The metal may be brought to a flat point like a chisel or to a square point, like an elongated pyramid but the forging process is essentially the same.

TAPERING SQUARE BAR

With the end of the bar at a yellow heat, hold it at a slight angle to the face of the anvil, hit once or twice then twist the bar through 90 degrees, hit once or twice again, return to the original position and repeat. It is not necessary to rotate the bar to hit all four sides. By twisting the wrist, the bar can be turned through 90 degree without needing to change your grip. This principle is important. Finding a comfortable grip that allows the wrist to be rotated accurately through a 90 degrees angle is the key to keeping the bar truly square in section. Practising with a piece of cold square bar and twisting it from one face to another, can be time well spent. It may also be helpful to lodge the hand against your leg to steady the bar while you hit it.

Remember you only need to hit two adjacent sides. The blows should be straight and solid, not wiping along the bar. Hammering on one side crushes the bar and makes it thinner but wider. Twisting the bar through 90 degrees allows the wider side to be crushed in turn. The net effect is to reduce the section and displace the material along the bar, increasing its

length. To bring the bar to a point, it should be positioned so that the tip of the work is always at the far edge of the anvil. For a square point the breadth and width of the bar are worked evenly. For a chisel point the bar is worked more in one plane than the other, so that the breadth is tapered while the width is kept parallel.

OPPOSITE PAGE: Elegant umbrella and hatstand by John Creed. Long tapers carefully planned before bending.

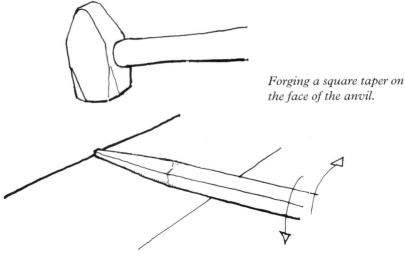

Forging a square taper on the face of the anvil.

Positioning the end of the taper at the edge of the anvil gives the hammer access to forge the tip.

In this position, the hammer may hit the anvil, not the end of the taper.

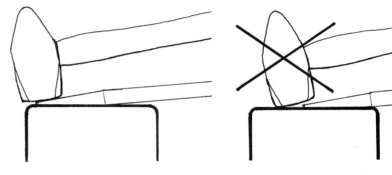

Correcting a section that has gone out of square.

BELOW: Forging a short taper first, to avoid splitting the end.

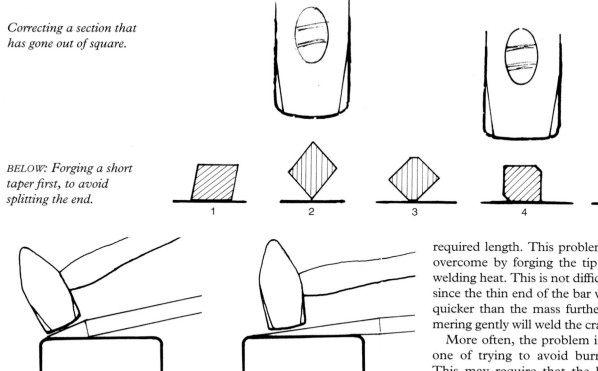

If a square bar is not rotated accurately through 90 degrees each time, it can quickly develop into a diamond section and then very easily become twisted or flattened. This is a tendency to watch for. If caught immediately, it is easy to correct the section by turning the longer axis of the diamond vertical and giving it a few blows, then resuming the proper alignment. If this is done before the metal is too close to its finished size, the proper square section can be re-established.

The internal movement of the metal – being alternately crushed in two directions at right angles – produces stresses that can cause the end of the bar to split. For this reason, no matter how long the desired taper, it is better to begin by forging an abrupt taper, almost to the finished size at the tip. This will reduce the tendency of the bar to split at the end. It can then be forged further back to increase the taper to the required length. This problem may also be overcome by forging the tip of the bar at welding heat. This is not difficult to achieve, since the thin end of the bar will heat much quicker than the mass further back. Hammering gently will weld the crack.

More often, the problem is the opposite one of trying to avoid burning the end. This may require that the bar is pushed through the hot centre of a coal or coke fire so that the vulnerable tip protrudes from the other side. Or the tip may be quenched in the water tank, to cool it before continuing to heat. So long as you are forging mild steel, this will not harm the metal, but it should be avoided with carbon steels.

In the course of forging a taper the bar will invariably bend and need to be straightened, and the regularity of the taper will need to be checked. Sighting along the bar will allow you to locate and assess both these things (*see* page 30) The bar may be straightened by holding it on the anvil face with the peak of the bend uppermost, and hammering down. The position of irregularities in the taper should be noted and forged to a clean line. It is always good practice to keep the bar as straight as possible and not to let it get out of control. It is a workshop truism that 'the work should look good at every stage', and this is certainly worth striving for.

Always remember that in making a point on the end of a bar, you have just produced

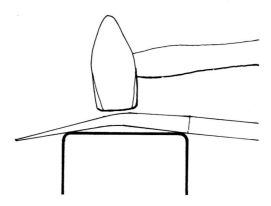

Straightening a bar.

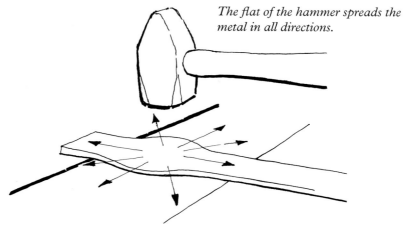

The flat of the hammer spreads the metal in all directions.

a potentially dangerous spike. Never leave it in a position where you can walk into it.

USING A CROSS-PEIN HAMMER

It is helpful to understand how the metal moves. A blow from the the flat of the hammer makes the hot metal spread in all directions. As we have seen, to taper a bar with the flat of a hammer, the breadth and width are crushed, in order to extrude the length. But by using the cross pein end of the hammer, the metal may be controlled to move more particularly in one direction. The cross pein digs in, displacing the material. In this way a bar may be spread in length or width, as desired. This principle can be applied to drawing down, by taking a yellow heat and placing a series of blows along the bar to stretch it. Placing more blows towards the tip will thin that end.

The flat of the hammer is used to smooth out the corrugations and irregularities, to finish the taper. Having to use the flat of the hammer to, as it were, repair the damage might seem to be time wasted, but tapering this way can be a lot quicker.

This process of 'notching' the metal is called fullering. The same effect may be achieved by working the metal with the flat of a hammer over a rounded edge of the anvil, over the bick, or by using a fuller

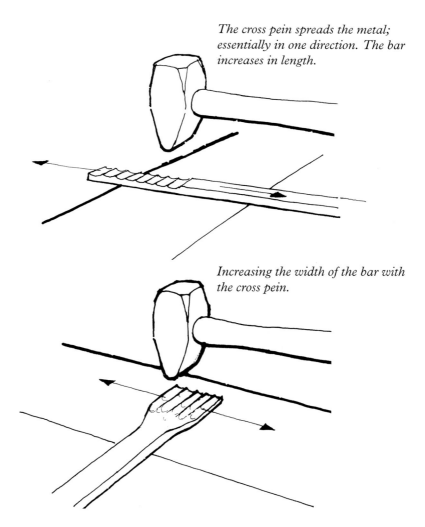

The cross pein spreads the metal; essentially in one direction. The bar increases in length.

Increasing the width of the bar with the cross pein.

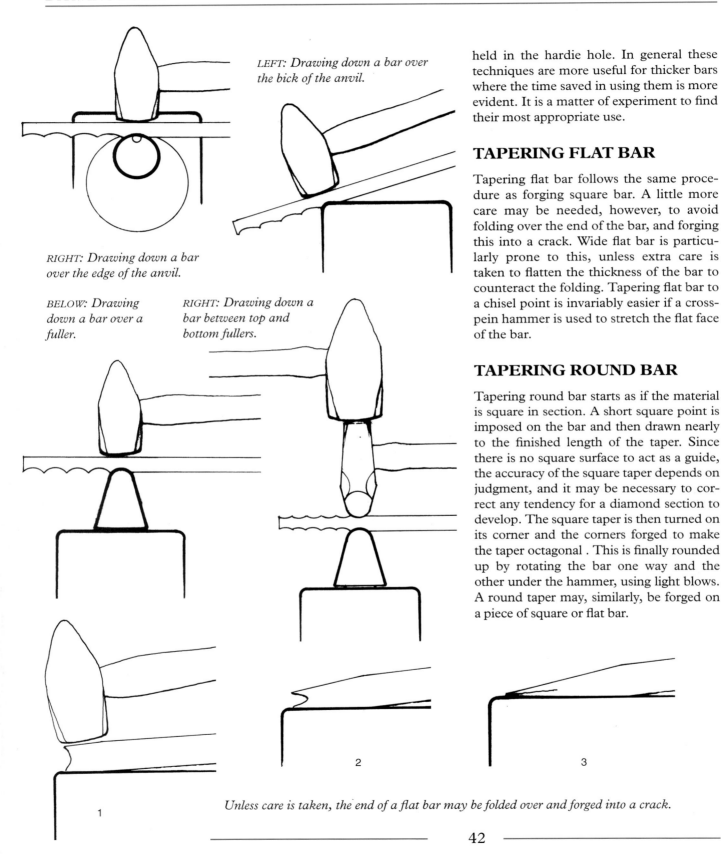

LEFT: *Drawing down a bar over the bick of the anvil.*

RIGHT: *Drawing down a bar over the edge of the anvil.*

BELOW: *Drawing down a bar over a fuller.*

RIGHT: *Drawing down a bar between top and bottom fullers.*

1

2

3

Unless care is taken, the end of a flat bar may be folded over and forged into a crack.

held in the hardie hole. In general these techniques are more useful for thicker bars where the time saved in using them is more evident. It is a matter of experiment to find their most appropriate use.

TAPERING FLAT BAR

Tapering flat bar follows the same procedure as forging square bar. A little more care may be needed, however, to avoid folding over the end of the bar, and forging this into a crack. Wide flat bar is particularly prone to this, unless extra care is taken to flatten the thickness of the bar to counteract the folding. Tapering flat bar to a chisel point is invariably easier if a cross-pein hammer is used to stretch the flat face of the bar.

TAPERING ROUND BAR

Tapering round bar starts as if the material is square in section. A short square point is imposed on the bar and then drawn nearly to the finished length of the taper. Since there is no square surface to act as a guide, the accuracy of the square taper depends on judgment, and it may be necessary to correct any tendency for a diamond section to develop. The square taper is then turned on its corner and the corners forged to make the taper octagonal . This is finally rounded up by rotating the bar one way and the other under the hammer, using light blows. A round taper may, similarly, be forged on a piece of square or flat bar.

Stages in forging a round point.

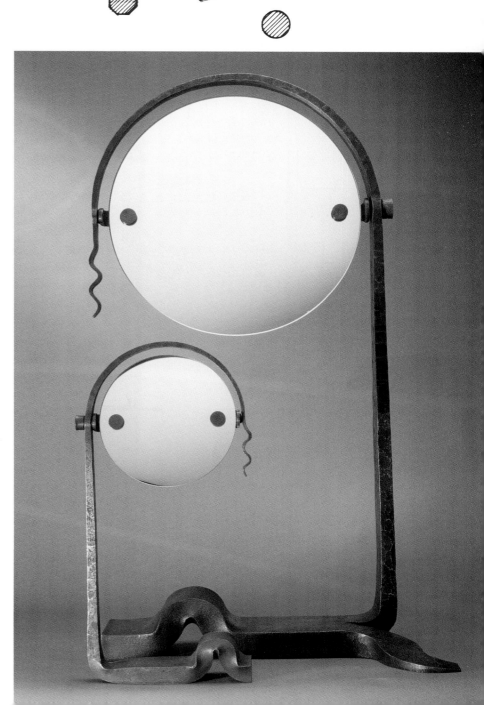

HAMMER MARKS

The pattern of finishing blows will give a round taper a very particular appearance. The blows may be placed close together giving a finely figured surface, or further apart to show distinct facets. Either way, the hammered surface looks quite different from the surface of the stock rolled bar, and this is equally true for square or flat sections. The question therefore arises whether the whole bar should be hammered to unify its appearance.

The great German smith, Fritz Kuhn writing in the middle of the last century, talked of hammering the bar all over to make it 'his' metal. Having, for example, drawn down one end of a square bar he would continue to heat and hammer over the remaining plain portions. Not, it should be said, to give it some kind of 'rustic' appearance, but to imprint it with his character and personality. Contemporary German smithing owes a great deal to this philosophy – the aesthetic of the hammer mark.

Traditional British smithing has tended to take the opposite approach of avoiding any extraneous hammer marks. It can also be argued that if the hammer marks are a record of the actions employed to shape the metal, then it is more honest to leave alone the parts that do not need to be hammered. There is no definitive answer, each case is different and in the end the choice is yours.

MEASURING AND CALCULATING TAPERS

Since a taper 'grows' on the end of a bar, it makes sense as a matter of routine to measure and note the length of the bar before

Mirrors by the author, with long tapers drawn down from a split, heavy bar.

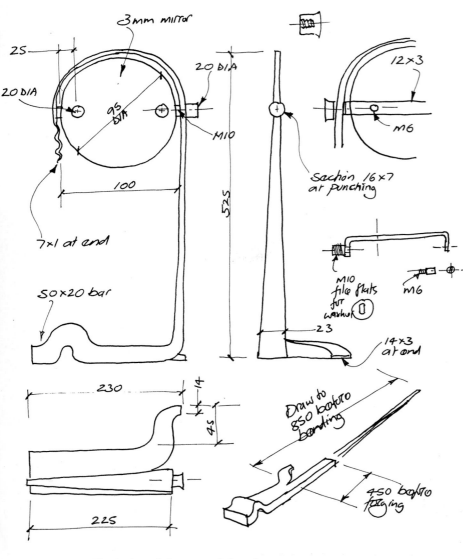

ABOVE: Typical workshop record drawing.

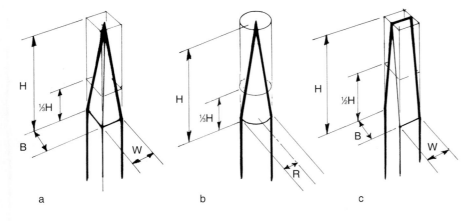

you begin forging. Once you are satisfied that the taper is as you want it, the bar can be measured again. The increase in length is the crucial dimension. Noting the length of the taper and the 'blank' required to produce it is important information and worth keeping for future reference. Making notes as you work, albeit simply chalked on the floor or on the hood of the forge, is a good habit to develop. These notes can form the basis for information kept in a project file to enable you to make another similar piece of work. Even if the original intention is to make a single item, you may burn off the end, you may subsequently want to make more, or you may wish to modify the original design. In each case, notes made of the stock size, length of taper and so on, are vital.

Making a component that tapers from one end to the other is straightforward. It can be forged on one end of a bar and cut off. But it is often necessary to forge both ends of the bar to produce the required piece. This means predicting the length of bar needed to forge the other end, in order to cut it at the right point.

The material needed to make a particular forging can be established by calculating the finished volume of material and working back, to find out what length of stock bar this volume represents. For those with an arithmetical mind, this enables a whole variety of forms to be analysed as geometric solids and the length of stock determined. But happily for plain tapers, application of the formulae result in very simple rules of thumb. The stock needed to produce a given length of chisel-ended taper on square or rectangular bar is half

Calculating tapers.
a) Volume = $\frac{1}{3}H \times B \times W$. A square point H long can be forged from bar $\frac{1}{3}H$ long.
b) Volume = $\frac{1}{3}H \times \pi R^2$. A round point H long can be forged from bar $\frac{1}{3}H$ long.
c) Volume = $\frac{1}{2}H \times B \times W$. A chisel point H long can be forged from bar $\frac{1}{2}H$ long.

the length of the taper. The stock needed to produce a square point on square bar, or a round point on round bar, is one-third the length of the taper.

This assumes that in each case the taper is drawn to a sharp edge or point and that the profile is truly straight. It also assumes that the flow of metal is perfect, and that none will be lost in the form of scale. In practice there is usually a discrepancy and it may be necessary to add 5–10 per cent to the theoretical length.

ASYMMETRICAL TAPERS

It may hardly need saying, but to produce an asymmetrical taper, it is easier to make it symmetrically first of all, then forge it out of line to finish it. When drawn on paper the two forms may look quite different, but the difference is just a slight sideways

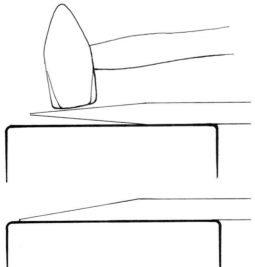

displacement of the end of the bar. For this reason the same rule of thumb applies to calculating the length of material.

ABOVE: Well grille by Charles Normandale, showing a pattern of hammer marks used to express the shape of the well.

LEFT: Setting over a taper to make it asymmetrical.

STEPPED TAPERS

A taper may start from a step in the bar. This can be achieved with smaller bars by taking a good yellow heat, setting the bar carefully on a suitably radiused edge of the anvil and driving down with hammer blows that overlap the edge. The bar may be stepped in two planes if required. For the first blow or two, it may help to hold the bar at a slight downward angle to ensure that the corner of the anvil notches positively into the hot metal at the right place. Once established, this notch will serve to locate the bar against the edge of the anvil while the taper is worked as already described. The reduced section may be kept parallel, if desired.

With larger material it is easier, and offers more control, to make an initial notch with a top fuller, laying the yellow hot bar on the

BELOW: Sequence showing a taper drawn down from a fullered groove. Note the length of taper drawn from the short fullered section. Charles Normandale, part of a fixing for his frieze in Chartered Accountants' Hall.

flat of the anvil, then draw the taper from the notch. In this way the bar may be notched all round and the bar drawn down square from the fullered groove.

FORGING A LEAF

A taper need not be at the end of a bar. By positioning a portion of the bar beyond the far edge of the anvil and forging a small notch as just described, a taper may be forged away from the notch in either direction. A classic application of this technique is in the forging of a leaf. A short taper is forged on the end of the bar, then the bar is held over the far edge of the anvil, where there is a radiused edge, and driven down in two planes to produce a neck. The effect of this is to isolate a short piece of bar on a stem. This short piece is the blank that will become the leaf. Both the stem and the blank can be refined in shape before flattening the blank to produce the leaf. The form of the blank dictates the shape of the leaf. In this way a variety of leaf shapes can be produced.

ADJUSTING LENGTHS

Since the length of a bar increases as it is drawn down, this effect can be used to adjust its length to fit a particular dimension. This is particularly useful where, for example, both ends of the bar have already been forged, or two holes have been punched a little too close together. Taking a red heat on a square bar and hammering it for a little way along two adjacent faces, may be all that is needed to lengthen it. If more adjustment is needed, another heat should be taken further along the bar. By judicious use of this process, a bar may be increased in length by quite a considerable amount without showing signs of becoming significantly thinner.

If a bar is already too long it can be shortened by upsetting, which is described in Chapter 7.

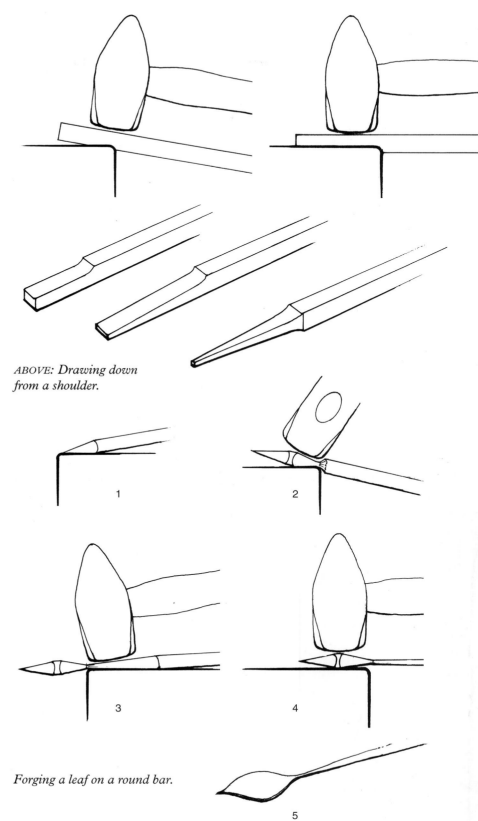

ABOVE: *Drawing down from a shoulder.*

Forging a leaf on a round bar.

6 BENDING

MEASURING AND MARKING

Usually all the forging to change the section of a bar is completed while keeping it straight, and it is only bent to shape at a final stage. It is far easier to taper, punch or spread a bar while it is still straight, since the bending may make access impossible to some parts. This means that the position of these features must be carefully planned so that they finish in the proper location after the bar has been bent.

One of the simplest ways to measure curves on a drawing is to use a piece of white, plastic-coated electric flex or washing line laid on the drawing to mark off significant points with a soft lead pencil. With the flex straightened out, these dimensions can be chalked on the bar, on a piece of steel plate, the floor, or the face of the anvil, as required. Marks on the flex are easily erased so that it can be reused the next time. If a forged prototype has already been made, the flex can be similarly laid along the metal to plot the positions of significant details.

For many purposes, a chalk mark may be sufficient to locate a bend. Chalk marks are invisible on a yellow hot surface, but at red heat they can be seen well enough. It may be useful to make a mark a little distance from the bend point, where the metal will not be so hot, and line this up with a mark on the anvil. Checking the dimension from the end of the bar before completing the bend can allow its position to be adjusted where necessary. If a precise mark is unavoidable, it can be made with a

centre punch on the side of the bar, but will remain visible after the work is complete. A similar mark made on the inside of the bend may be less easy to use, but closes up as the bend is made. Avoid marking the outside of the bend, since the punch mark will be stretched by the bending, making it even more prominent.

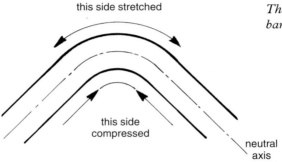

It is important to understand that when a bar is bent, the outside of the bend is stretched while the inside is compressed. This effect can be quite clearly seen if a short heat is taken near the middle of a square bar and the two ends pulled together, to create a 180 degree bend. The outside of the bend narrows and the outer face becomes concave, while the inner sides are widened and the inner face bulges. In between these two extremes, the centre line of the bar is considered to be a 'neutral axis' that is neither stretched nor compressed. It is the only part of the bar that retains its original length. Measurements taken with a piece of flex over a drawing, or a prototype bent bar, must therefore be taken along the centre line – the neutral axis.

OPPOSITE PAGE: Delicate free bending by Brian Russell. An entrance arch to a new housing development.

The effect of bending a bar.

BENDING ON THE ANVIL

There are a number of different ways of bending a bar. The most direct is by taking a good red heat, longer than the bend required, holding the bar over the edge of the anvil and striking it at a point beyond the anvil – in thin air. Working over the bick, the bar should be placed square to its curve. The anvil provides a point of support and the hammer provides the leverage. It should be emphasized that this is quite a different action from forging to draw down a taper, where the bar is sandwiched between the hammer and anvil. Even the sound is different. If a long heat is taken on the metal, free curves and waves can be made very quickly. This is the most spontaneous way of creating flowing curves, and offers a quality of freshness that is hard to achieve by other means. A bar may also be curved by holding it with one end resting on the anvil face while striking the hot bar to make it bend, working on the inside of the bend.

Free bending over the bick.

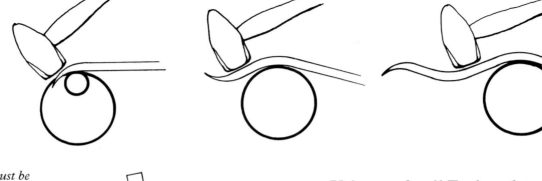

RIGHT: The bar must be square to the curve of the bick.

BELOW: Bending a bar by direct hammering.

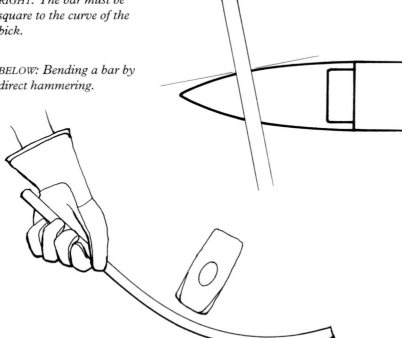

Using an Anvil Fork and Scroll Wrench

Free curves and bends may also be made using an anvil fork that fits the hardie hole, together with hand-held scroll wrenches. The anvil provides an immovable point so that the bar can be secured in the anvil fork and pulled to shape with a wrench, or by applying leverage between two wrenches. Moving the metal bit by bit through the fork and pulling a little each time can produce long, sweeping curves, but care must be taken not to produce kinks in the bend or to mark the bar. The stability of the anvil is a limitation to this technique and care must be taken to avoid pulling it off its stand by applying too much leverage, when bending a long or heavy bar.

When making bends in this way it is always important to look critically at the bar and correct any kinks or lumpiness in the curve. Good free curves can look beautiful, but poor ones can look just that. The eye is remarkably sensitive to the smoothness of a curve, so it is worth spending a little time on it. If the curve goes badly wrong, it may well be better to straighten the bar and start again. So long as the bar is always worked at red heat, no harm will result from bending, straightening and re-bending.

Right-Angle Bends

If more precision is required, the metal may be dressed down over an appropriate part of the anvil to reproduce the required bend or curve. Hammering the bar in thin air produces a sound that changes abruptly the moment it makes contact with the anvil. At this point, stop hammering or the metal will be needlessly crushed.

Bends can be hammered over a radiused edge of the anvil and dressed down to a right-angle, assuming the side is truly at 90 degrees to the face. It would seem logical that a bend could be accurately located by holding the bar on the anvil face, with the start of the bend level with the edge of the anvil, then hammering the hot metal over the edge. But in practice the bar is inclined to be dragged over the edge by the hammering action, moving the position of the bend. The answer is to place the bar a little further back initially to counteract this tendency, or to bend it first to a larger radius over the thin end of the bick or a soft edge of the anvil face. The bend position can then be adjusted one way or the other and sharpened by dressing it down in the correct place.

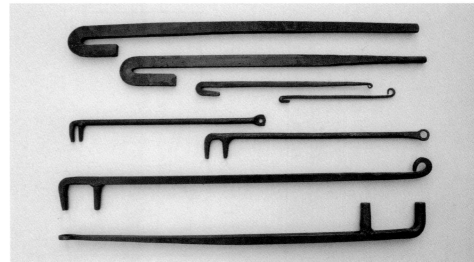

TOP: Bending bar by using an anvil fork and scroll wrench.

ABOVE: Twisting wrenches (top); scroll wrenches (bottom).

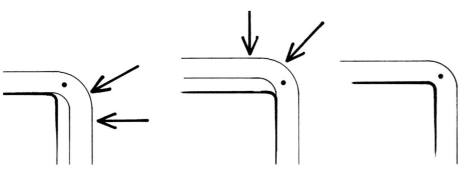

Moving a bend to the marked position.

Hammering the hot metal over an edge of the anvil pushes the far end down but the resulting bend tends to lift up on the near side of the point of support. If you are working by yourself, this will require the occasional correcting blow, hammering down again before bending the bar further. If available, have a helper hold a heavy sledgehammer on the bar, while you hammer over the end and this will reduce the problem.

Round or square bar may be bent easily, as indeed flat bar can be bent on the flat.

Bending flat bar on edge, however, becomes more difficult if it is very wide in relation to its thickness. The inner and outer edges of a bend are subject to considerable stresses, stretching on the outside of the bend and compressing on the inside, so the wider the bar the greater is this effect. The bending must be undertaken with care, paying particular attention to forging the flat face at the outside of the bend to help the metal stretch, and hammering accurately on the edge of the bar to avoid twisting.

Making a forged bend.

BELOW: Bending a ring over the bick.

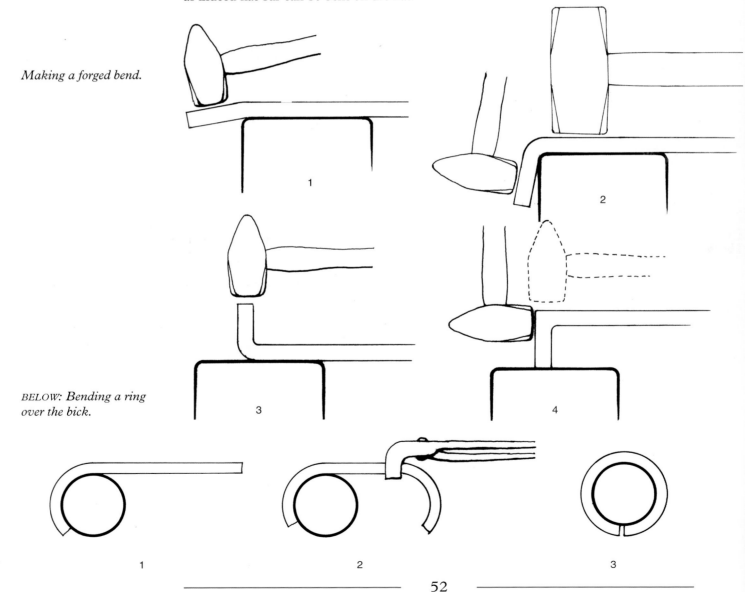

Forged Bends

There is a natural limit to the bend radius that can be achieved on any given section. But a bend may further be forged, to square up the radius of its corners, by driving in metal from either side of the original bend. This is called a 'forged bend'. It is crucial in this operation to take a yellow heat on the bend and avoid pinching the metal between hammer and anvil, which will reduce its thickness. Since the action is essentially to upset metal into the corner, a longer, heavier length of bar is easier to work than a short, thin piece.

Making Rings and Eyes

Rings may be made by using the bick of the anvil as a former. Each end of the bar should be worked over the bick first, then the ring closed up on the face of the anvil, and finally dressed truly circular around the bick. A loop or eye may be made on the end of a bar

THE MAKING OF AN EYE.
ABOVE LEFT:Forging an initial bend.

ABOVE: Starting the eye by forging the end back the other way.

LEFT:Rounding up the eye over the bick.

*THE MAKING
OF AN EYE.*
ABOVE: Closing the eye.

*ABOVE RIGHT: The
completed eye.*

USING THE HEAT

The smoothness of a bend relies to a large extent on the metal being at an even temperature where it is bent. The metal will by a combination of techniques. Self-evidently, if the bick of the anvil is not truly circular, it will be more difficult to produce good circular rings.

always bend where it is the hottest, no matter where the pressure is applied. So the heat must be in the right place. Sometimes the best kind of even heat is to leave the bar completely cold. As long as the required bend is not too tight, thinner bars and long sweeping curves may be better bent without heating at all. A cold bar can be curved by striking where it bridges over a hollow in a swage block. By striking the bar with consistent force and moving it along between blows, a smooth regular curve or ring can be formed. The principle of supporting the bar at two points while striking in between, can also be used to curve a bar by hammering it over the hardie hole, over the step in the anvil, the open jaws of a leg vice or even over pieces of scrap bar laid on the anvil face.

The exact length of the heat can also be used to control the radius of a bend. A short heat will give a sharp bend with a small

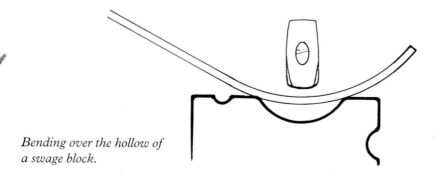

*Bending over the hollow of
a swage block.*

radius while a longer heat will give a softer bend of a larger radius. Isolating the heat by quenching at either end, or by heating with a torch, allows a bar to be bent by securing one end in a vice or locating it in a hole in an anvil or swage block while pulling the other end by hand. If the heat length is measured and chalked on the metal, repeat bends may be made in this way, with reasonable accuracy.

BENDING IN A VICE

Using a leg vice allows the position of the bend to be located and the bar pulled round and hammered square onto the side of the jaws. The bar can also be clamped in the vice cold, in the correct position for the bend and then heated with a torch as close to the vice jaws as possible. This can work well enough for smaller sections but the vice itself absorbs large amounts of heat and may prevent the bar being heated close to the jaws. It can be better to heat the bar first, then locate it accurately in the vice using chalk marks. Since a chalk mark is impossible to read on yellow hot metal, it should not be placed at the bend point, but further back where it will be visible. It can then be lined up with the far side of

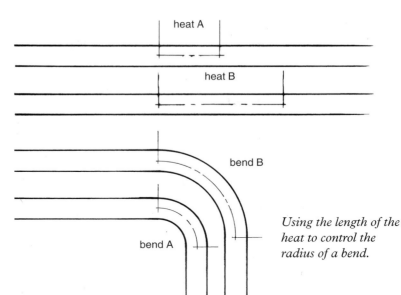

Using the length of the heat to control the radius of a bend.

the vice or a chalk line on the jaws. Bending in the vice allows bends to be placed with predictable accuracy.

Short ends of square and flat bar can be used as formers to space right-angle bends, to make, for example, a 'U' shape with an accurate spacing between the uprights. Using loose pieces of bar in this way allows a number of repeat bends to be made accurately and is a short step from making a

Bending in a vice. Note the chalk marks locating the bend.

Cross finials for a church balustrade.

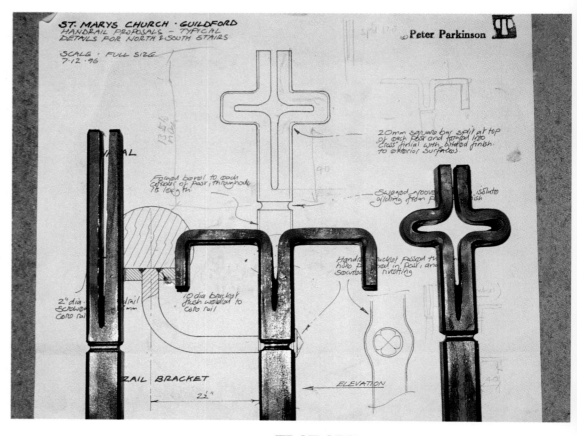

ST. MARYS CHURCH · GUILDFORD
HANDRAIL PROPOSALS – TYPICAL
DETAILS FOR NORTH & SOUTH STAIRS

SCALE · FULL SIZE
7·12·96

©Peter Parkinson

OPPOSITE PAGE: Entrance gates by Alan Evans. A multitude of bends made with special top and bottom tools.

special bending tool or jig. Securing a loose piece of bar against the workpiece in a vice can be fiddly with just two hands, and even very simple devices can help. A small scrap of thinner bar can be tack welded to the former or two short pins can be driven into drilled holes, to stop it falling between the vice jaws.

BENDING WITH SPECIAL TOOLS

An anvil provides the means to make bends and rings up to the full diameter of the bick, but an accurate ring of a larger size requires a larger forming tool and repeated bends need a more accurate tool. These kinds of tools belong to the category of 'repetition tools' that are dealt with in more detail in Chapter 14.

FLAT SPIRALS

A bar may be rolled into a flat spiral by first bending the end tightly over the edge of the anvil then gently hammering the curl back in the direction of the parent bar, to encourage the bar to roll up on itself. The initial bend is crucial since it provides the form over which the rest of the bar is rolled. The bar, in effect, becomes its own forming tool. Two bars can be laid side by side and rolled round together. Separating these bars gives two flat open spirals.

The flat spiral may be left alone or, for example, flattened (*see* page 10). A flat spiral may also be pushed out to form a shallow cone by taking the whole spiral to an even red heat, laying it over an appropriate circular hole in a swage block and gently tapping the centre down using a ball-pein hammer or a suitable punch.

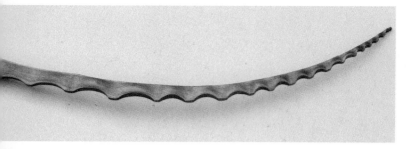
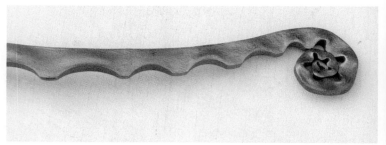

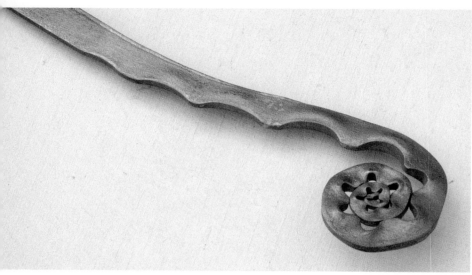

A FLAT SPIRAL BEING ROLLED UP ON ITSELF.

ABOVE LEFT: *The bar has been tapered and hammered over a fuller. The curve is simply the result of the displacement of metal during fullering.*

ABOVE: *The tip is bent over the edge of the anvil and tucked in.*

LEFT: *The developing roll is hammered gently back to wind it up.*

A flat spiral may also be produced by bending the end of a bar to a right-angle, securing this in a vice and winding the remaining bar around the stem. This is far easier using a heating torch.

Scrolls and other repetition bends are dealt with under Bending Tools in Chapter 14.

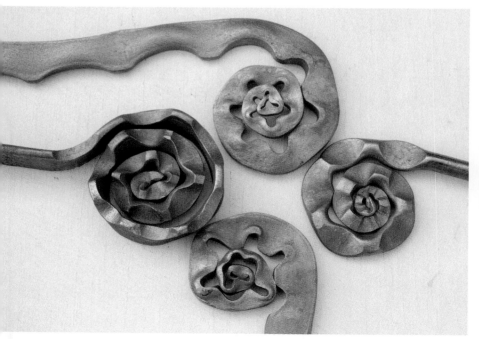

Variations on a theme.

Curtain pole finial by Miranda Souter. A conical spiral made by dishing a flat spiral.

THE MAKING OF A FLAT SPIRAL CANDLEHOLDER.

TOP: *(Left to right) The initial flat bar; the end tapered; the other end spread; right-angle bend; spiral pulled round; tail cut off.*

ABOVE: *Pulling round the spiral in a vice jig. A flat surface is needed to dress down the flat bar if it buckles.*

RIGHT: *Candleholders with copper and brass pans, by the author.*

7 UPSETTING AND SPREADING

Upsetting is in effect the opposite of drawing down. A bar is upset in order to thicken it locally. A good yellow heat is taken and force applied to the end of the bar, to drive metal together, thicken the bar and reduce its length. Since the metal moves the most where it is the hottest, control of the heat is particularly important to ensure that the bar is upset in the right place. Upsetting can be used to bring metal to the end of a bar to create a knob or handle, make the head of a rivet or provide a mass of material as a starting point for forging some other form. It can similarly be used to increase thickness in the middle of a bar, to provide more metal for a punched hole, forged corner or some other detail.

There are a number of methods of upsetting, but in each case the problem is maintaining the straightness of the bar during the process. For this reason it is more difficult to upset, say, a piece of 8mm round or square bar than 16mm bar. It might be easier still to upset the end of a piece of 25mm bar. Different techniques are needed for different sizes.

UPSETTING THICKER BAR

The end of a length of bar should be heated to as bright a yellow as you dare, the bar held vertically and the hot end pounded down on the flat of a swage block, an anvil on the floor, or a suitable block of scrap metal. At the first sign of bending, the upset end must be forged straight on an anvil. Taking a very short heat and rotating the bar during the process helps to equalize the

bending problem. It can also help to upset the bar in the first heat, then forge a short bevel on the end. This serves to centralize the force of the blow and keeps control of the sharp flared edge of the upset end. If a large upset is required, this can be repeated. The weight of the bar provides much of the impact so it is better to upset a long length, then cut it to size afterwards.

A bar may similarly be pounded down on the face of the anvil, paying due attention to light fittings overhead. A shorter bar can be upset by holding it vertically on the anvil and either hammering the hot end directly, or driving it down on the anvil face with heavy hammer blows on the other end. The bar may be held in a gloved hand, or in tongs. A longer bar can be held level over the edge of the anvil and struck horizontally with a hammer, supporting the other end on a stand if necessary. The mass of the bar itself provides the resistance allowing the metal to be upset, so again the effectiveness of this technique depends on the weight of the bar.

Pounding the end of a bar on a surface, or striking it directly with a hammer gives a slightly different result. Pounding a bar tends to produce a longer, gently flared form, while hitting the metal directly tends to give a shorter, more abrupt flare. Different weights of hammer also produce different results. A lighter hammer will affect just the immediate end of the bar, flaring it abruptly, while a heavier hammer will deliver sufficient impact to move the metal further back from the end, resulting in a longer flared form. The length of the heat will nevertheless have an overriding effect.

OPPOSITE PAGE:
Gate posts, delightfully sprouting leaves, by Steve Lunn.

Leg of a coffee table by the author, showing 25mm (1in) bar upset by pounding on a block.

To upset a bar at some intermediate point it is essential to have a short intense heat in exactly the right place. This can be achieved by taking a heat and swiftly quenching back at either end, over the water tank, to isolate the area of yellow heat. This calls for deft action. The bar may then be upset by the methods already described. If the bar is pounded vertically, the longer part should be above the heat to provide weight. If the end of the bar is hammered directly, the shorter part should be hammered. In this case it can help to support the bar vertically by dropping it into a hole in a swage block with the bottom end resting on a block on the floor. The upper part of the bar can then be held straight with a gloved hand while blows are delivered to the end. Whether the bar is worked horizontally or vertically, it can help to rotate it during the process to equalize errors. The moment it begins to bend it should be straightened over the anvil.

UPSETTING THINNER BAR

Very thin bar, say 8mm (5/16in) or less, needs to be held horizontally in a vice, to avoid slipping, with little more than its own diameter protruding from the jaws. A very short heat is essential and it is hard to work quickly enough to take the metal from fire, locate it, tighten the vice and hammer the end, before the bar is too cool. A lighter hammer helps, since repeated blows can be delivered more quickly. Round bar is very liable to be driven back in the vice by the hammer blows. Grips can be made from two short pieces of flat bar, clamped with a piece of thin card in between and drilled edgewise to the diameter of the round bar, to provide two semi-circular false jaws. An oxyacetylene or oxy-propane heating torch is a great asset in upsetting thin material, since heat may be applied to the bar while it is already clamped in the vice. The bar will still buckle very easily and needs constant attention to keep it straight.

Upsetting a thin bar at some intermediate point is helped even more by heating with a gas torch. Taking a heat in a fire and quenching back is almost impossible to achieve with sufficient speed, since thin material cools so quickly. It is also more difficult to avoid bending the bar when upsetting it near the middle. A gas torch offers an almost immediate way of heating the bar while it is already clamped in the vice. Small bars can, however, easily be straightened over the hardie hole. The upset bulge lies in the hole, while the bar at either side is lined up by the anvil face and hammered true.

FAR RIGHT: A neat gate latch, by Charles Normandale, showing upset knob handle.

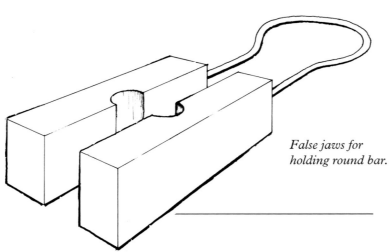

False jaws for holding round bar.

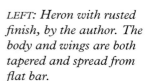

LEFT: *Heron with rusted finish, by the author. The body and wings are both tapered and spread from flat bar.*

ABOVE: *Heron, detail. Marks from a cross-pein hammer used to spread the flat bar.*

SPREADING

As mentioned in Chapter 5, a cross-pein hammer offers directional control when spreading metal. A bar can be flattened and spread, to make a wide flared end, a leaf or some other feature. The fullering action of the cross pein enables the metal to be moved in one particular direction, with little displacement in the other direction. Metal can therefore be shaped more directly than by using just the flat of the hammer.

Since the size of the parent bar dictates the maximum width of spread that can be achieved, upsetting the bar provides more material, allowing the spread to be wider. So, for example, a larger leaf might be made from the same size of bar. This can be a quicker method than the alternative, which is to start with a larger bar and draw it all down, leaving just a short piece of the original section at the end.

Despite (or perhaps because of) the physical nature of the craft, blacksmiths are concerned to save time and energy. So deciding whether to take a thick bar and draw down most of it, or to take a thinner bar and upset part of it, is an important choice. If you have a power hammer, drawing down the thicker bar may be a perfectly viable approach. But doing it all by hand,

can require a lot of time and energy, so upsetting may be a better choice.

Door latch by Peter Crownshaw. The metal has been both spread and tapered. Note the fine tapered end used to provide spring pressure on the latch bar.

8 HOT CUTTING

Cold metal may be cut by a variety of methods – sawing, shearing, guillotining, gas-cutting, plasma cutting, laser cutting and so on. But the most characteristic way in blacksmithing is to hot cut the metal with a chisel.

CUTTING WITH A HARDIE

Cutting with a hardie has already been mentioned in Chapter 4, and this is perhaps the most frequently employed form of hot cutting. It is used to cut off lengths of bar, or to cut a forged component from the end of the parent bar. The simplest way is to locate the hot bar on the cutting edge and give it a series of vertical blows. As the hardie cuts through, it will chill the thinning section of metal and show a dark line over the cut. Watch for this line and stop hammering the moment it appears. You do not want to cut through the bar and drive the hammer face onto the hardie, blunting it. It is also very easy to abruptly sever a red hot end and send it shooting across the workshop, to disappear in some inaccessible corner. So when a dark line is visible, the remaining thin web of metal should be bent backwards and forwards to break it.

The hardie may be forged symmetrically and be sharpened by grinding both faces evenly. In this case, cutting right through from one side will leave the cut bar with angled faces. The hardie can, however, be forged and sharpened so that one face is vertical and the other ground at an angle, like a wood chisel. The resulting cut will then be vertical on one side and angled on the other. By placing the hardie the required way round, the component can either be cut off with a square or an angled face.

By rotating the bar over the hardie, it may be cut through progressively from all sides. So a flat or square bar can be nicked on all four faces or a round bar cut all round. Care is needed to rotate the bar so that the cuts line up around the bar. Again the very last few blows must be light, in order not to damage the cutting edge of the hardie.

CUTTING WITH A CHISEL

More precise hot cutting is achieved using hot chisels. These may be directly hand held, or fitted with steel rod or timber handles, in which case they are known as 'set chisels' or 'hot sets'. Set chisels are intended to be struck with a sledgehammer swung by a striker, while the smith holds the workpiece and the tool. But they can also be used if you are working by yourself if the workpiece can be suitably supported. Set chisels have a distinct advantage in cutting large sections, since they keep the hand away from the hot metal, and allow the smith to deliver a few blows with a heavy hammer.

The metal may be cut and left, or it may be cut in preparation for further forging. In design terms, cutting may be an alternative to bringing bars together. A wide bar may be split into three branches, or three bars may be brought together and welded into one. The end result may look quite similar. Complex forms can be cut and split out of one piece of bar, then forged, rather than being put together from smaller parts.

OPPOSITE PAGE: Hot cutting with a hardie.

An elegantly simple crucifix by Charles Normandale, made by hot cutting the bars.

The way the cutting edge of the chisel is ground can leave vertical or angled faces. If the edge is subsequently to be forged over, this may not matter. But if the cut edge is to be left, it may be worth grinding the chisel specially to produce a particular result.

Cutting a bar along its centre line is a classic use of the process to make, for example, a toasting fork or some decorative split detail. In this instance, it is better to use a chisel ground symmetrically and with the edge a slight convex curve. The wedging action of the sharp end serves to split apart the two halves of the cut. It is easier to lay the bar lengthways on the anvil and sight along it from the end, in order to position the chisel centrally. Starting with the end of the bar facing away from you, and leaning the chisel away from you, locate it on the centre of the bar. One blow will mark the end. The chisel can then be rocked towards you, still located in the cut, paying attention to sighting its near corner on the centre of the bar, and hit again.

Sliding and rocking the chisel in this way means that it need not be lifted out of the groove as it is moved and there is less risk of making unconnected or multiple cuts. Each time the chisel is moved, its further corner remains located in the cut already made, so you simply have to concentrate on ensuring that its near corner is on the centre of the bar. The chisel should, however, be taken out and cooled in the water tank after every few blows to prevent the edge overheating.

It is easier to lay out the whole length of the cut with the metal at red heat since the surface can be seen clearly, then take a yellow heat and cut right through. Before the chisel breaks through, a piece of scrap sheet steel (or scrap non-ferrous metal) should be placed underneath the workpiece to protect the cutting edge of the chisel from being blunted on the face of the anvil. With a sharp chisel a bar may also be cut through directly from one end, while holding it vertically in a vice. This works better for short cuts and has the advantage that the end of the cut has the same appearance on both sides.

Once the bar is split, the two halves may, if necessary, be splayed apart a little, either by hammering down each end or by levering them apart around the sides of the hardie. At a good red heat, one leg may then be folded back to lie over the parent bar while the remaining leg is forged to shape as required. The forged leg can then be folded back, and the other one pulled straight to forge it in turn. It is important to fold back each leg sufficiently to give access to the end of the cut in order to forge over the feather edge of metal left by the chisel. It is easier to cut through flat bar in this way, than through square or round. So if a split is needed in square or round bar, flatten it first until it is at least twice as wide as its thickness. The flat portion can then be split far more easily and neatly.

It should be remembered that once the two halves of the split have been forged, only the near end of the cut will remain visible, so it is important that it is neatly in the centre of the

GREZZO   SEMILAVORATO   FINITO

Three stages of hot cutting and forging a flower from one piece of flat bar, by the highly skilled Italian smith Angelo Bartolucci.

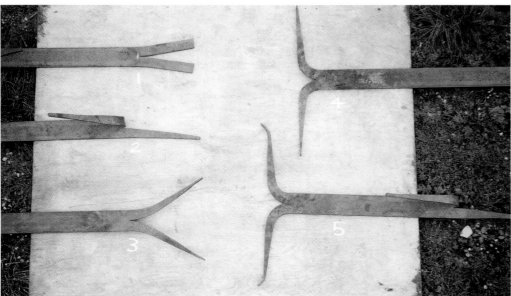

Stages of cutting and forging part of a window grille. (Anti-clockwise from top left) the bar split; one leg folded back to taper the other; both legs forged; the legs forged back into a straight line; the tips curved.

Stages in forging units for the same grille. (Left to right) the cut marked; one end split and forged, and cut off the bar; both ends forged and checked for size and alignment in a jig; the forging bent to a 'U' shape in a fly press tool.

bar. But If the rest of the cut wobbles a little, it does not matter since this will be obliterated.

The purpose of the cut is to separate two masses of metal. In the case described, two equal masses. But the cut need not be central on the bar and need not be parallel with its edge. A cut can be angled so that it ends on the centre line of the bar, but splits it into two unequal masses. These can then, for example, be drawn down into two tapers of unequal length.

Cuts may be made into the side of the bar as well as the end, allowing branches

to be pulled out. It can be useful to do this using a curved chisel to start the cut. Curved chisels may also be used to provide decorative cuts, or to profile a shape out of the hot metal.

CUTTING HOLES

Rather than punching a hole, a chisel can be used to make a slit through a bar that can be opened up and drifted through to make a hole. Holes produced in this way can be of any desired size, depending on the length of the cut. It is possible, for

The effect of splitting and drawing down.
1) Cut along centre line.
2) Cut offset to one side.
3) Cut at an angle.

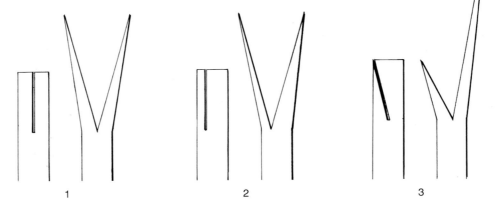

example, to make a hole through flat bar, far larger in diameter than the width of the bar.

A large slit can be upset, fitted over the bick of the anvil and the bar hammered around the outside of the hole, to forge in the feather edge left by the chisel cut. In the same way, if the chisel cut terminates close to one end of a bar, the short stub of bar left at the end can be forged in to leave a perfect loop. Indeed, taking the cut close to both ends of the bar makes it possible to forge a circular hoop, without welding.

A chisel can also be easier for making holes through fairly heavy sections of tool steel, to make the eye of a set tool. Since the chisel is cutting though a considerable mass

of hot steel, it is important to be able to extract it quickly to cool it, so it should have a good taper to prevent it sticking. The hole should also be cut from both sides of the bar. The effect of this, together with the use of a tapered drift, driven in alternately from each side, is to leave a neck in the hole, which helps to secure the timber shaft of the tool. Chisels, fullers, swages and hammers can all be made in this way (*see* Chapter 14).

Cutting a hole through a flat bar with a chisel.
1) Chisel cut.
2) Bar upset to open out the cut.
3) Hole forged over the bick and the short tail forged in, to make a smooth ring.

BELOW: Detail of the hot-cut tongue construction of gates for the V&A Museum, by Jim Horrobin. Each tongue is finally riveted to the other bar.

1   2   3

9 PUNCHING

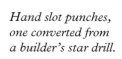

Drilling a hole removes material, while punching essentially does not. Hot punching moves the metal plastically so that very little is removed. Its engineering virtue is that the strength of the bar is maintained, while its aesthetic virtue is to provide an expressive swelling in the bar where the metal has been displaced. A 12mm (½in) drilled hole through the centre line of a 25mm (1in) wide bar leaves only 6mm (¼in) at either side. But punching the same size hole through a 25mm (1in) bar will leave at least 10mm (⅜in).

Punches are ideally made from tool steels containing chromium, the better to resist the effects of rapid heating and cooling, but are often converted from old cold chisels, 'star' chisels or forged from salvaged motor car torsion bars or vehicle coil springs. For rigidity, they should be forged and ground from fairly substantial bar, perhaps 20mm (¾in) across, with a short but gently tapering end, ground and finished smooth. The tip of the punch is flat, but some smiths prefer to grind them to a shallow cutting edge like a blunt chisel, on the basis that this helps them displace the hot metal more easily.

PUNCHING THE HOLE

To punch a hole, take a good yellow heat on the bar, place it on the flat of the anvil and drive in the punch using heavy blows. To preserve the end of the punch, it should be withdrawn and quenched every so often. Drive the punch in quickly until it stops. It will have trapped a thin skin of metal between the tip of the punch and the face of the anvil. Withdraw the punch, flip over the bar and you will see a dark outline where the skin of metal has chilled against the anvil. Quench the punch, locate it on the dark mark and drive it in again, still working on the face of the anvil. As the punch enters the metal, it will shear off the thin skin. The bar and punch are finally slid over the pritchel hole of the anvil and the punch driven in a little more gently, to eject the thin skin of metal and complete the hole.

All this takes far longer to describe than to achieve. You should aim to punch the hole in one heat, so it is essential to work quickly and decisively. Using a heavier hammer for this purpose is helpful. Since only a few blows are necessary you do not need to handle the extra weight for too long. It is crucial to embed the tip of the punch in the metal at the outset, so this calls for a sharp, heavy blow. You do not want the tip of the punch to wander around or make multiple impressions. If you have doubts about your ability to give a hard blow to a hand-held punch, use one with a handle, or hold the hand punch in tongs or a locking wrench.

Before heating the bar, the position of the hole should be marked quite deeply, using a centre punch. If the mark is not immediately visible when the metal is at a yellow heat, sliding the hammer or the side of the punch over the surface will scrape forge scale into the mark, revealing its position as a darker spot.

Hand slot punches, one converted from a builder's star drill.

OPPOSITE PAGE: Bollard by Alan Evans, showing the characteristic swelling around punched holes.

Round and slot punches with handles.

If a round hole is required on the centre line of a wide flat bar, say a 12mm (½in) hole in 50mm (2in) flat bar, a round punch can be used. There will be little swelling of the bar at the sides of the hole. But if the same hole is required in a piece of 25mm (1in) wide bar, substantial swelling will be required to maintain the thickness of metal at either side. This is best achieved using a slot punch that has a narrow, rectangular profile at the tip, like a screwdriver blade with rounded edges. The purpose of this is to create a long thin slot along the centre line of the bar, leaving as much thickness as possible at either side.

Alternatively, a wider swelling can be provided by upsetting the bar where the hole is required, then punching through the upset section.

DRIFTING A HOLE

Usually a hole is pierced initially with a punch, then finished to the required size and profile using another tool called a drift. Drifts may be made from round, square, or rectangular mild steel bar. A hexagonal drift can be useful for making spanners and an oval drift is useful in shaping the eye of hammers and set tools. Drifts may be made of tool steel for greater durability, but mild steel is normally adequate. If a series of holes is required to fit a particular size of bar, make the drift from a piece of the same bar. Eventually you will accumulate a collection of drifts to suit all the standard stock sizes. A typical drift has a short parallel body that is the profile of the original bar, a long taper at the working end and a short taper at the other. The drift is hammered on the short tapered end, the taper

BELOW: Punching a hole with a slot punch – end view.

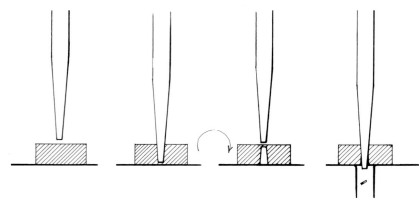

Drifting a hole.
1) Hole slot punched.
2) Hole after upsetting.
3) Finished hole after drifting.

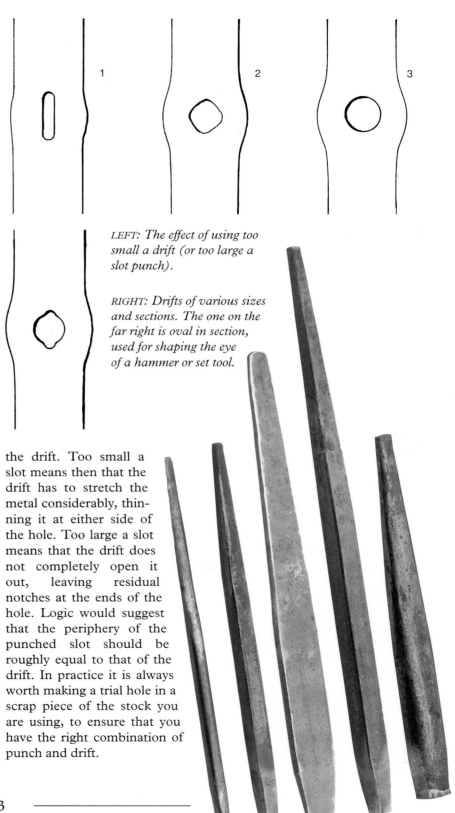

LEFT: *The effect of using too small a drift (or too large a slot punch).*

RIGHT: *Drifts of various sizes and sections. The one on the far right is oval in section, used for shaping the eye of a hammer or set tool.*

serving to ensure that the burr produced by the hammering does not foul the hole as it passes through. The taper needs to be longer than the thickness of the workpiece, to make sure that the parallel body of the tool can be driven clear. The long taper should be small enough at the tip to enter the punched hole.

If a rectangular hole is needed, it is necessary to punch the initial hole using a slot punch. The rectangular drift then serves to stretch the hole slightly and refine its shape. If the initial slot is punched quickly, the rectangular drift can be driven into the hole immediately, otherwise another heat will be needed. Working over the pritchel hole, drive the drift in part way. Withdraw it quickly by lifting the bar with the drift embedded in it, resting the tip of the drift on the anvil and striking the bar close to it. Flip over the bar, insert the drift again and drive it right through. Quickly dress down the raised edges of the hole on the flat of the anvil, and drive the drift through again, to give the hole its final shape.

The drift should be hit carefully as it exits the hole. It can be ejected quite suddenly from the other side of the bar with enough force to stick in a timber floor. Keep your feet out of the line of fire and ease off for the last few blows.

A hole initiated with a round punch can be finished with a round or square drift. But if a good swelling is required on the sides of the bar, it is preferable to start the hole with a slot punch. For the maximum swelling, the bar should then be upset at the slot, until it becomes a round hole. The drift then simply smooths the profile of the hole, with very little stretching.

There must be a relationship between the size of the slot punch and the size of the drift. Too small a slot means then that the drift has to stretch the metal considerably, thinning it at either side of the hole. Too large a slot means that the drift does not completely open it out, leaving residual notches at the ends of the hole. Logic would suggest that the periphery of the punched slot should be roughly equal to that of the drift. In practice it is always worth making a trial hole in a scrap piece of the stock you are using, to ensure that you have the right combination of punch and drift.

Supporting the Bar

As the drift passes through the hole, the hot bar needs as much support as possible to avoid distortion. Sometimes the pritchel hole is too small and the hardie hole is too big. A hole is needed that is only a few millimetres bigger than the drift. One answer is to use a bolster that is simply a piece of thick flat bar pierced with a series of different-sized drilled holes. This is placed over the hardie hole. Alternatively the workpiece may be positioned over an appropriate hole in a swage block while the hole is drifted through.

PUNCHING THIN OR THICK BARS

Punching a hole through thin bar, say 3–4mm thick, can be difficult because the bar cools so quickly. This is more testing to your speed and dexterity than punching a hole through material twice as thick. Using a heavy hammer, placing the hot metal quickly on the anvil and even working on a hot anvil can all help. (Heat a heavy flat piece of bar in the forge and lay it on the anvil face for a minute or two.) The thin bar will almost certainly need to be supported on a bolster to prevent it buckling when the hole is drifted.

Very thick bar retains its heat, but also heats up the tip of the punch to the point where it begins to bend or upset slightly and stick in the metal. To prevent this happening, it is particularly important, to withdraw it frequently and quench it between blows, and to ensure at the outset that it has a good clean taper.

SPACING PUNCHED HOLES

Since the bar can be stretched or upset in the course of making holes, some allowance must be made if a series of holes need to be spaced accurately. This is typically a problem when making a gate, railing, screen or grille with parallel vertical bars. If the vertical bars are tenoned into holes in top and bottom rails any discrepancy in the spacing will show, because the verticals will not be parallel.

Marking them out directly from the drawing and punching in that position, may give inaccurate spacing and result in a significant change in the length of the bar. An error of 2mm between each pair of holes, may in itself seem insignificant, but will accumulate to 20mm over ten spaces. If the piece of work does not need to fit a particular space, this may not matter. But if the finished size is critical, an adjustment is necessary in the marking out.

The answer is to accurately mark out, then punch and drift three trial holes in a piece of scrap bar of the same section. The bar should be cooled, the hole centres can then be measured and the appropriate adjustment made to the marking out. It is very important that the finished bar is punched and drifted in precisely the same way as the trial piece. Each successive hole should receive the same treatment. Don't suddenly change punches, or decide to jump up the punched hole before drifting, part way through a series of holes. It is also good to set out the holes using a pair of dividers, to ensure that they are equispaced and mark them deeply with a centre punch. This is more accurate than marking off each position from a steel rule.

It may also be thought that some error would be due to the expansion of the metal when hot. Indeed, a 1m length of mild steel will expand some 10mm at red heat. But when cooled down, will of course revert to its original length. Since the metal is measured and marked out when cold and ends up cold after it has been forged, the effect of expansion and contraction cancel each other out and can therefore be ignored.

After each hole has been drifted, the bar should be checked and straightened, before punching the next hole. All the holes should be punched from the same side. Finally the hole positions can be checked and if any have moved, the bar in between can be adjusted by heating and jumping up to reduce the dimension or by hammering to stretch it.

CUTTING HOLES

Holes may also be made by cutting. Using a chisel the bar can be split along the centre line and the cut opened out to make a hole to any required size. This is dealt with in more detail in Chapter 8.

PUNCHES FOR OTHER PURPOSES

In addition to making holes, punches can be used for other purposes. A flat ended punch can be used to make a recessed area to take a fixing. This might be on the centre line of the bar or partly overlapping the edge, to push out an 'ear' of metal. A fixing hole can subsequently be drilled or punched through the recessed area, to accommodate a screw or rivet.

Punches may be used for decorative effects. You can make your own punches, forged and ground to any number of profiles to provide a means of imprinting patterns into a hot metal surface. The mark produced may be negative or positive. Punch marks can be used singly or in groups to create a pattern or to texture a complete surface. It should, however, be borne in mind that each punch mark displaces metal, so that a series of imprints can distort the outline of the workpiece to a surprising extent. In the right situation this distortion can provide a decorative and expressive detail, but if you are wanting to maintain a straight edge or fit the punched component to another, take care.

Fire tools by Paul Margetts, showing rivets in punched recesses.

In general decorative punches can provide a point of emphasis (*see* Chapter 14 Hand Forging Tools).

Letter and number punches are commercially available in a variety of sizes, and can be used to mark steel, hot or cold. These are useful for marking components for assembly so that, for instance, the right bar goes through the right hole. It can also be useful to mark templates and tools you have made with information such as dates and sizes.

BELOW: Marking punches, used to decorate and mark work.

RIGHT: A Valentine token using the heart punch (see photo above).

BELOW: Mirror frames by Shona Johnson, one gilded, the other silver leafed. The metal has been punched all over to texture the surface.

RIGHT: *Punching used to make one of seventy faces applied to existing primary school railings, by Brian Russell.*

BELOW: *The punch the author uses to mark his work, applied to some fire tools.*

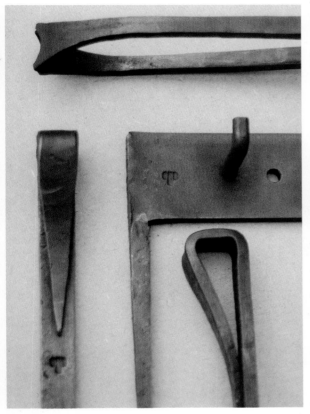

There are firms that specialize in making punches, from your artwork, to reproduce lettering or any kind of pattern. These punches can be expensive, but since they are able to reproduce the most complex detail, they can pay for themselves in producing a result that you could not make in any other way. Many smiths use a name punch or symbol to mark and identify their work. This could be produced by such a firm, or you may wish to design and make a mark or symbol punch yourself. This is a worthwhile project in its own right since it gives your work a special identity.

10 TWISTING

The twisting of metal wire and bar for decorative purposes has been in use since ancient times. Twists were used to decorate bronze and precious metals long before they became part of the vocabulary of traditional blacksmithing. They are a simple way of giving decorative emphasis to part of a bar and can be very expressive of the plasticity of the metal.

The process is simple. A heat is taken on the bar, one end is gripped horizontally in a vice, a wrench is applied to the other end and the bar quickly twisted. If the bar is long, it helps to support the end on a stand, close to where the wrench is applied. It is important to take an even heat and isolate the hot length by quenching at each end, so that there is a sharp cut-off between the hot and cold portions. This ensures a precise start and finish to the twisted part of the bar. If the metal is simply taken hot from the fire and twisted, the heat will fade into the cool bar at either end, the hottest part will twist the most, giving a sloppy uneven twist. An even heat will give an even twist. Any square, rectangular or flat bar can be twisted in this way.

It is good practice always to count and note the turns as you make a twist, and to line up the faces of the two plain ends, rather than stopping the rotation at some arbitrary point. This information makes it possible to reproduce the twist, or to make a tighter or looser twist with some measure of control. In practice it is also quite difficult to count the turns of a twist by examining the result afterwards, so counting as you go is a good habit to develop. So long as it is at a good bright heat, a bar may be

twisted an extraordinary number of turns before it finally shears off. It is a matter of experiment and judgement to decide how tight or loose to make the twist.

The metal moves the most where it is the hottest, so it follows that neither the vice nor the wrench need to hold the bar near the place where it is to be twisted. In fact since the visual effect of the twist depends on crisp sharp edges, the wrench is best positioned well away from the hot part of the bar. Should the twisting action cause the bar to bend, it must be straightened with great care, using a metal hammer only on the cold, plain parts of the bar. The twisted portion may, however, be hammered directly with a rawhide mallet, without marking the metal. Take a good red heat, place the bar on a timber block and hammer the twist

Twisting a bar.

OPPOSITE PAGE: Three 35mm (1⅜in) diameter bars twisted together to make 'rope' bollards, by Chris Brammall. Hot dip galvanized finish.

ABOVE: *Straightening a twisted bar, using a rawhide mallet on a wood block.*

RIGHT: *Making the end of a twisting wrench by folding a bar over a packing piece.*

There is a tendency for these tools to bend the bar as it twists, since the load is applied from one side. For this reason, some smiths prefer to make twisting wrenches with two handles, or adapt the kind of tools described by welding on another handle. Since these apply a more balanced twisting action, they are less likely to bend the bar. A two-handled wrench may also be made by welding short scraps of, say 16mm bar, as spacers between two opposing handles, to leave a 16mm square hole. But like a box spanner, this type of wrench may only be fitted over the end of the bar to be twisted, while the 'J'-shaped wrench can be applied from the side, at any point along the bar.

Forging the Bar before Twisting

Treating the bar, or just part of the bar, in some way before twisting can have a dramatic effect on the appearance of the twist. The bar may simply be tapered then twisted. In general, the more linear details – edges or grooves – forged on the bar, the more visually complex will be the result. A square bar may be forged on its corners to give it an octagonal section, a round bar may be forged to a hexagonal section, bars may be cut with a chisel, fullered to make grooves or imprinted with a punch along one or more faces. A square bar may be twisted, forged back to a square section then twisted again. Bundles of bars – for example two round and two square – may be tack welded together at the ends or even bound together with wire to allow them to be twisted as if they were one bar, producing a composite twist. The square bars in this composite could themselves have already been twisted before forming part of the bundle and being twisted together with the round bars. Despite the essential simplicity of the process, there is plenty of room for experiment and innovation.

Consider the effect of groups of twisted bars. The direction of the twist is important. Bars placed close together will look

with the mallet, just as you would straighten a bar on the anvil.

Twisting Wrenches

Some form of wrench is necessary to grip the metal firmly while it is twisted. Traditionally these are made by folding back the end of a length of square or rectangular bar to provide a 'J'-shaped tool to fit a particular size of section. The tool is bent over a scrap piece of bar to give the correct size. These work well so long as the tool is made from a bar of the same, or a little larger, section than the metal being twisted. If rectangular bar is used it should be bent on edge so that the wider dimension takes the leverage. A mechanic's adjustable wrench used for nuts and bolts can also work well, so long as the jaws are smooth and reasonably wide to avoid marking the bar.

quite different if the twists are all in the same direction, or if alternate bars are in opposite directions.

Reverse Twists

A bar itself may be reverse twisted, using short sections of clockwise and anti-clockwise twist alternately. Take a heat and quench it at each end to isolate a short length with a good even colour. Twist, then quench the twisted portion and take another heat immediately adjacent to the twist and quench at either end to isolate it. Twist again in the opposite direction. The process is then repeated to produce the required length.

Making reverse twists can be neater and easier if you use a heating torch, since the bar can stay secured in a vice throughout. The length of each twisted segment can be

ABOVE: Twist samples. (Top to bottom) eight sides forged on a square bar and reverse twisted; round-edged flat bar twisted; flat bar twisted; square bar cut with a chisel and twisted; plain twist on square bar; the twisted bar reforged square; the bar retwisted.

LEFT: Four twisted 50mm (2in) flat bars, make a detail in a box section column for a floor standing lamp, by Alison Rew.

measured and marked out with chalk before twisting. One end segment is heated and twisted, then quenched by pouring water from a can and catching it in another. The next segment is heated and twisted the opposite way, and so on. The effect of reverse twisting on some of the more complex sections mentioned above can produce wonderfully rich results, but a word of caution is appropriate.

There is a seductive simplicity about twists that tends to encourage beginners to twist absolutely everything. But the visual drama of a twist is often heightened by using it sparingly, in contrast to larger areas of plain forged bar. You can indeed have too much of a good thing. The great German architect Mies van der Rohe is credited with the adage that 'less is more', and this is never truer than with twists.

Using a small section of twist as a point of decorative emphasis can have far more effect than winding whole lengths of bar into a continuous twist (*see* photograph, page 153). It should be remembered that much of the magic of a twist lies in the sense that it is part of the same plain piece of bar. It has more impact because the viewer is aware of the transformation. The point of change is the critical area. After a lot of work, a long continuous twist may prove to be disappointing and read simply as a texture.

Twisting Tube

Tube may be twisted, but will easily collapse. Handled well, this can become a very decorative feature. By selectively heating the tube with a torch, it may be twisted in specific places. Square tube can be twisted with a round bar passed down the centre to act as a mandrel and stop it collapsing. This can be difficult to remove and may even need to be left in place. Round tube can alternatively be used as a mandrel where an electric wire is to be fed down the tube to make the stem of a lamp.

OPPOSITE PAGE: Flat bar twists used to great effect in the main entrance gates to Hackney Community College, by Matthew Fedden.

'Chromatic Pegs'. A coat rack by John Creed, featuring a wonderfully understated twist.

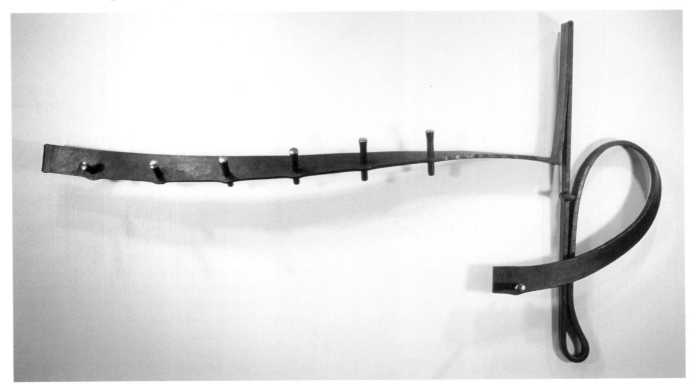

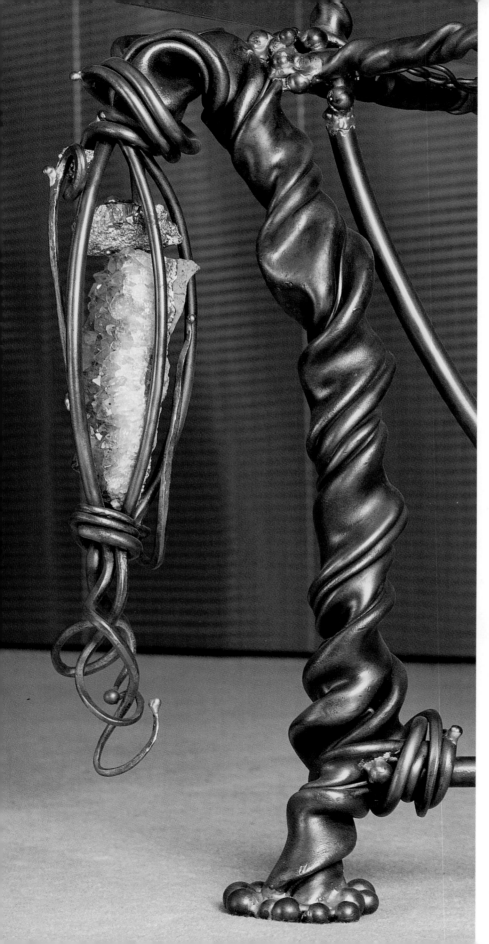

Detail of 'Lobster' dining table, by Shelley Thomas, showing richly twisted tube.

Straightening Bars

For some applications square or flat bar may need to be untwisted. Stock bars as delivered, often have some degree of twist already present, and it is easy to inadvertently impart some twisting in the course of forging the bar. This may not be immediately apparent, but reveals itself when lengths of bar are assembled to make, for example, some kind of square frame like a gate, railing, or screen.

It is easy to check square bar by securing one end in a vice, supporting the other end on a stand and laying three short lengths of bar crosswise on its top face. These short pieces – perhaps 250mm long – are called 'winding bars'. Place one at either end and one in the middle. Sighting along these bars will clearly show any twist, and a wrench used to remove it. If the winding bars at either end are out of line, the centre bar should be moved along to see if the twist is continuous from one end to the other, or begins at some intermediate point. In this way the twisted portion can be identified and straightened, by applying the vice and wrench at either end.

Wide flat bar should not be held by its thin edges for twisting. It will almost certainly spring, rather dangerously, out of the vice. The bar can be laid on top of the vice and stand, checked with the winding bars, and the appropriate points chalk marked. With its flat faces safely secured in the vice, it can then be twisted as necessary. However, it may be simpler in the long run to secure the bar with its flat faces in the vice, and fix the winding bars against the flat of the bar, using small clamps. Sighting along the winding bars as they stand vertically, the wrench can be applied and the bar untwisted and checked again, keeping the winding bars in place.

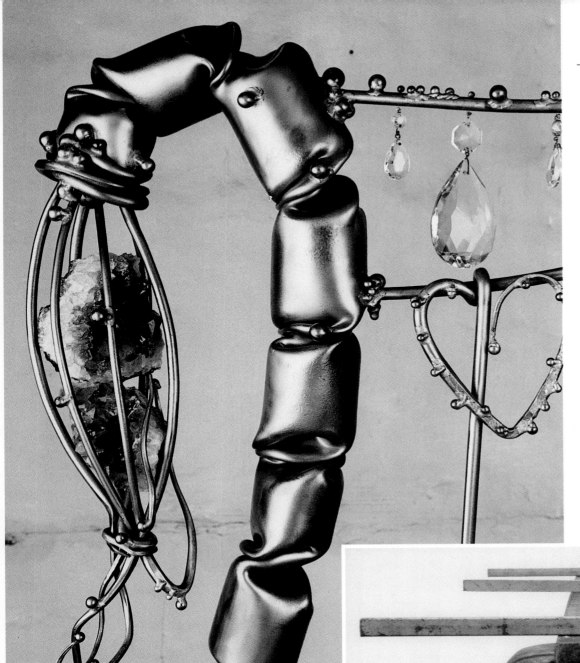

BELOW: Checking the twist in a bar, using winding bars.

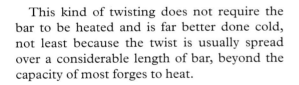

This kind of twisting does not require the bar to be heated and is far better done cold, not least because the twist is usually spread over a considerable length of bar, beyond the capacity of most forges to heat.

11 JOINING PROCESSES

Joining processes are of great importance to the blacksmith. Although some pieces of work may be made from one piece of metal, the majority require separate components to be joined together, often in considerable numbers. The way in which the joints are made can be a major design feature. Contemporary German smithing has characteristically made impressive use of the joint as 'decoration'. Interesting and expressive joints, rather than serving simply to hold together a decorative structure, have themselves become a major element of the design. The philosophy is – don't apologize for a necessary detail, make it a feature.

FIRE WELDING

Until recent times this was the only welding method available to blacksmiths. Both gas and electric arc welding only became generally available around 1900. The great French artist blacksmith Edgar Brandt, began making use of both processes just after the First World War. Since that time, considerable development has taken place and electric welding has evolved into a number of discrete processes for different applications. Most of these have been readily taken up by blacksmiths, so with such a choice, the use of fire welding is, perhaps not surprisingly, less widely used than in years gone by. Wrought iron is somewhat easier to weld than mild steel, while carbon steels are more difficult.

Fire welding, also called 'forge welding', involves the heating of the iron or steel components in the fire, until their surfaces becomes molten. If the two surfaces are placed together they will stick and fuse completely when struck with a hammer. This means that the metal is joined across the whole of the interior of the completed joint. In gas or arc welding, unless the metal is thin, fusion only takes place at the surface affected by the torch. So special preparation of the metal is often necessary to ensure that the weld penetrates enough to ensure the strength of the finished joint. For this reason it should not be thought that fire welding has been superseded by newer, better methods. Each has its own advantages and applications. The characteristic branched, fire-welded joint in traditional running scroll work is virtually impossible to achieve in any other way.

Joint samples, showing different connections between a cross bar and an upright.

OPPOSITE PAGE: Detail of fire welds in the construction of an intricate window grille for Lincoln Central Library, by Brian Russell.

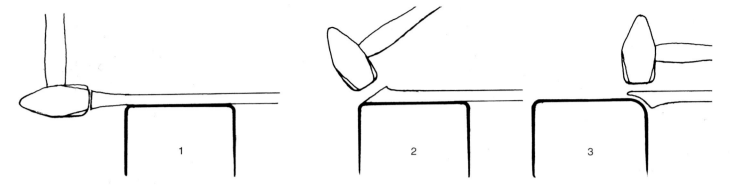

Scarfing a bar for fire welding.
1) Upsetting.
2) Angling the scarf.
3) Refining the scarf.

Preparation

Preparation of the metal is also usually necessary for fire welding. At welding heat the metal has both a fragile, molten surface and a very soft internal structure. It is easy therefore, to crush the material and thin down the bars unnecessarily while completing the joint. For this reason, bars are usually prepared by upsetting at the point to be joined, to compensate for the thinning of the bar during welding. Butt joints, where one bar is joined end-on to another, also call for the upset ends to be scarfed. That is, to be forged to create an angled surface that serves to locate the bars together and increases the area of contact. This kind of weld is one of the most difficult.

It is also important that the two surfaces to be brought together are forged to a slightly convex form. The purpose of this is to ensure that the centre touches first and the oxides and slag on the surface can be ejected from the edges of the joint as it closes, rather than being trapped. It should be noted that heavy hammering is not required. Just sufficient force should be applied to close the joint and eject the slag. Some smiths talk of 'shutting' the weld. Going on hammering will not weld the joint if the initial contact did not stick.

MAKING A WELD

In Britain, fire welding has traditionally been undertaken without flux. After preparation, the metal is heated to yellow heat in the fire and the pieces rapidly removed, vigorously wire brushed and returned to the fire. At yellow heat the oxide that sticks firmly at red heat, becomes loose and can easily be removed, leaving just a thin coating. As the metal reaches the proper temperature, a few sparks will be seen emerging from the top of the fire. At this point the pieces are removed, shaken as you might flick paint from a brush, brought together and hammered to make the joint. As blows are struck, molten oxide will be thrown out of the joint in spectacular fashion. For this reason it is vital to wear protective glasses and clothing, preferably including a leather apron. Warn other people if necessary. This is one of the most anti-social of all smithing processes.

In America it is routine to weld all joints using flux. The flux is anhydrous borax, or some combination of borax and other materials. Borax alone seems to work perfectly well. The advantage of flux is that it forms a protective layer over the metal, lowers the melting point of the oxide and shields the metal from further oxidation. In practice this means that welds can be achieved at a somewhat lower temperature. To weld with flux, the joint is prepared and the metal brought to a yellow heat, taken quickly from the fire and wire brushed, the flux sprinkled on the hot surface, where it melts and the metal returned to the fire. Avoid breathing the borax fumes.

If you are using a gas forge or coal fire it may be possible to see into the fire and observe the fluxed areas as they reach temperature. At welding heat the flux looks

ABOVE: The ends of flat bars fire welded to create a bowl, by Mark Dyvig.

Detail of a seat with a marine theme by Steve Lunn showing fire-welded tentacles.

wet and the surface seems to crawl a little. Bring the pieces quickly out of the fire and complete the joint. In a coke fire, the metal cannot be observed directly, but with care the bars can be slid rapidly out, checked, and slid back again without harm. At welding heat the metal will be emitting a few, tiny bursting sparks. Welding carbon steel benefits from the use of flux.

All this takes far longer to describe than achieve. The process itself requires quick, decisive action and several factors need to be taken into account to achieve success. The initial preparation of the metal is important. The fire itself must be clean without any build-up of clinker and the metal placed in the fire should have the mating surfaces facing downwards to avoid contamination. (Coke or coal fires are better for fire welding, offering a small area of intense heat.) The fire needs to be hot enough. Some gas forges may not be capable of reaching welding temperatures. Both pieces of metal must be at the same temperature. Be patient when allowing the metal to heat. There is a temptation to throttle up the fan but this is a mistake, since more air causes more oxidation. Be quite clear in your mind what you are going to do and have the hammer ready. If you are using tongs, leave them on the bar while the metal is in the fire.

It is better to build confidence with easier welds, rather than try butt welding two bars together straight off. Two (or more) pieces of bar can be held in one hand side by side in the fire, until they reach welding heat, planted on the anvil and shut together, without needing to manipulate them into position or let go of the hammer. If at a bright red heat you bend your two welded bars apart near the weld, it will test the joint and allow you to bring the other two ends around and weld them together into a heart shape. Hold the first joint in tongs for the second weld.

Welding chain links is also good experience. Decide on the length required for each link and chalk reference marks on the anvil. Scarf one end of a handling length of 10mm or 12mm rod, chalk the length and cut off on the hardie. Take the cut length in tongs, scarf the other end and bend it round until the scarfs lie over each other. Set the scarfs close together but not so that they touch and trap debris. At welding heat the hammer blow will set both the surfaces together and complete the weld. The scarfs may be arranged to overlap on the side of the link, and the link welded on the face of the anvil, or in the other plane, requiring the link to be welded over the bick of the anvil. In both cases the link will need to be finished on the bick.

Welding a heart.
1) Two bars held in contact.
2) The bars welded at the end, reheated and pulled apart.
3) The two ends brought together in a heart shape.
4) The second weld made to complete the heart.

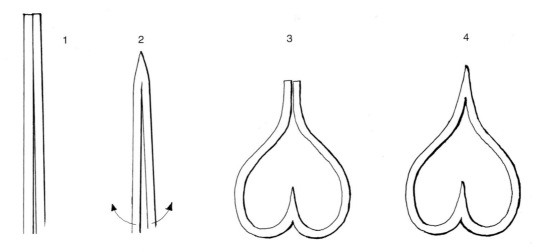

Butt welds require two separate pieces to be brought simultaneously to welding heat, removed from the fire, fitted together and welded. Prepare the scarfs on both pieces. If you are right-handed, the technique is to hold the longer piece in your left hand and the shorter in tongs in your right hand. Place your hammer ready on the anvil. Put the metal in the fire and bring it to yellow heat, withdraw rapidly, wire brush, flux if desired and return to the fire immediately, with the scarfs downwards. Bring up to welding heat, take both from the fire, flicking them or tapping them on the edge of the anvil to remove loose material then rest the right-hand piece scarf up on the far edge of the anvil and trap it with the other piece so that the scarfs lock together and stick. Drop the tongs immediately. The scarfed ends should still be angled together a little above the surface of the anvil, to avoid chilling, while you reach for the hammer and deliver a sharp blow or two, first to the centre of the scarf then the lip, flick it over and lastly hit the other lip of the scarf to ensure that it is welded before the anvil cools it.

Pattern Welding

Fire welding enables the smith to make his own material. Layers of iron and steel can be welded together to form laminations that can be made visible on the surface of the metal as a pattern like wood grain. This is sometimes referred to as 'Damascus steel'. Take a handling length of 30mm × 6mm (1¼in × ¼in) flat mild steel bar and lay a short piece of the same section of wrought iron and carbon steel on top of each other at one end of the bar, to form three layers. These should be 75–100mm long (3–4in). Tack them together at the near end using an arc welder, just enough to hold them.

This 'sandwich' can now be brought up to heat, fluxed and welded. If need be, use two welding heats to ensure that the whole

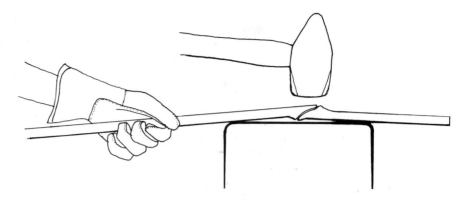

pack is fused into one block. It is important that the edges of the bars are welded cleanly in line and do not skew or overlap. The block is now drawn down to twice its original length, one half cut off and tacked over the other half, which is still attached to the bar. The welding process is then repeated, drawing down, cutting and restacking several times. Since each weld doubles the number of layers, they build up in the sequence 3, 6, 12, 24, 48, 96, 192 and so on. Six welds will make ninety-six layers, which may well be sufficient. Too many layers begin to blend and become less visible.

At this point the metal is like plywood with straight layers visible on its edges. Much of the interest in pattern welding steel lies in pattern development – methods of distorting the initial parallel laminations to produce complex patterns. The initial bar can be twisted, punched, cut, rolled up, made wavy, and so on. The surface can then be ground to expose the layers. Experimenting with layers made from different-coloured modelling clay can be useful in predicting patterns.

Three layers ready for fire welding, to make pattern welded steel.

Welding a butt joint. One scarf traps the other. Note the air gap below, preventing the metal chilling on the anvil until the hammer strikes.

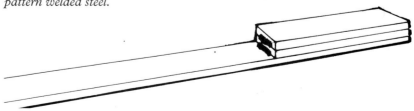

The patterned surface is finally revealed by grinding, filing and even polishing before lightly etching the surface with, for example, dilute nitric acid followed by wax finishing. Experiment is well worth while, to identify suitable pieces of wrought iron and carbon steel to give a good, clear contrast to the laminations. Pattern welding is a very demanding and laborious process. The patterns produced give the metal a wonderful richness that demands close inspection. For this reason the process lends itself to small and precious objects.

GAS AND ARC WELDING

See Chapter 15, More Tools.

RIVETING

Rivets have been used since ancient times and provide a way of making a secure joint, or a pivot between two or more surfaces or components. They have a decorative value which can give visual emphasis to the joint. Rivets are available as stock items in a range of metals, a variety of head shapes and in a wide range of diameters and lengths. Despite the supposed metrification of the engineering industries in Britain, a generation ago, iron rivets are still specified in imperial sizes. Rivets may be bought with a shaped head on one end of a plain shank, or may be made in the workshop.

The rivet is passed through holes in the work and the plain end hammered to upset it, make a head and lock the rivet in place, a process called 'setting'. Setting can be achieved cold if the tail of the rivet is simply

Pebble form made in pattern welded steel with brass inlay, by Peter Powell.

RIGHT: Detail of a wall mirror by the author, showing ten rivets used as decoration, where four would do.

flattened, or if it is heated, a shaped head can be forged so that both ends of the rivet are identical. Special heading tools – rivet sets – are needed to do this. One acts as a bottom tool to support the original head of the rivet and the other as a top tool, struck by a hammer to give the new head its finished form. The hot tail of the rivet must initially be hit with the flat of the hammer to upset it. Then the ball pein is used to strike around the edge of the upset head to forge it to a hemispherical form and the heading tool used to finish it. If necessary reheat the head with a torch to achieve this.

Rivet sets are available from engineering tool suppliers, may be found at car boot sales, or can made in the workshop. Heading tools can also be made to produce decorative forms of rivet head, such as conical, square, pyramid shaped and so on.

Making a Rivet Tool

To make a rivet set, first produce a hard steel punch, the tip of which has been filed or ground to the size and shape of the required rivet head. A short piece of tool steel bar, perhaps twice the diameter of the required head, is heated at the very end, locked vertically in a vice and the prepared punch driven down into its end, to produce the required depth of cavity. A locating mark with the tip of a drill can help to centre the punch initially. Metal will be drawn down around the punch, cupping the end of the bar. This will need to be ground or filed off to leave the shaped cavity just a fraction shallower than the full rivet head, so that the face of the tool does not subsequently make contact with the workpiece. The edges of the tool should similarly be rounded off. Harden it and temper to a purple colour. Bottom tools, used only to support the rivet head, are quite adequate made in mild steel.

Important Considerations

Setting rivets is a simple and reliable process, so long as a few basic rules are observed. The rivet must be a snug fit in the hole. If it is too loose, it will not initially be upset by the hammer, but will buckle in the hole. It is important that the first blows are struck solidly on the end of the rivet so that the whole length is upset and the diameter expands to grip the inside of the hole. The other end needs good support from a heavy vice or anvil. Care should be taken to ensure that the two pieces to be joined are in solid contact before the rivet is upset. Do not rely on the heading process to pull the two surfaces together. Commercial rivet sets have an additional clearance hole that is fitted over the projecting end of the rivet, so that the tool can be struck to drive the joint together. If possible, clamp the joint close to the position of the rivet before trying to set it, or use nuts and bolts in adjoining rivet holes.

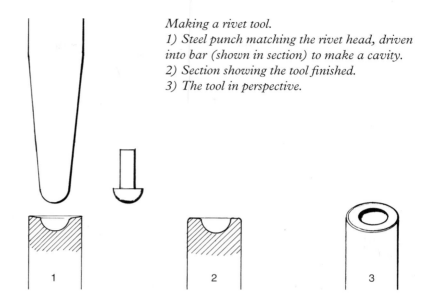

Making a rivet tool.
1) Steel punch matching the rivet head, driven into bar (shown in section) to make a cavity.
2) Section showing the tool finished.
3) The tool in perspective.

If the rivet is to be headed hot, try if possible to heat the whole length of the shank, not just the projecting tail. This will ensure that the body of the rivet is upset and the contraction on cooling will tighten the joint. Use loose rivets as pins to align the holes as the assembly is clamped. They can be removed one at a time, heated, reinserted hot and headed up. If the rivets must be heated *in situ*, heat the projecting end for a good time with a torch, to ensure that the heat has a chance to penetrate the length of the rivet. Do not leave too much of the rivet projecting. One and a half diameter's length provides enough material for a round head. If the rivet is too long, the end will buckle before the body of the rivet has been properly expanded in the hole.

Flush Riveting

Rivets may also be set flush, by forging the heads into countersunk holes. The holes can be punched or drilled in the workpieces to create the countersinks and commercial rivets obtained with countersunk heads. The countersunk head can be supported on the flat of an anvil while the tail of the rivet is headed, to fill the cavity at the other end. Plain short pieces of round

rod can also be used to make flush joints in this way, supporting the bottom end over spacers to allow enough projecting length to make the head. If the head is left slightly proud of the surface it can be ground or filed carefully, blending it into the parent metal to make it invisible.

Assembling with Rivets

It is crucial to provide solid support while the rivet is headed. This is easy enough to arrange if the assembly is small and portable, but if rivets are being set in a large structure, some ingenuity or help must be found to back up the rivet. If the work is being assembled on trestles, packing pieces can be arranged on an anvil dragged underneath to support rivets set vertically. Rivets set horizontally will need a helper to back them up with a heavy sledgehammer or a piece of steel bar. If necessary, a rivet head cavity can be punched specially into the end or side of such a bar, for this purpose.

Rivets do not always have to be round in section. A square bar can be used with advantage through square holes to make a single fixing to rivet together two components which might otherwise twist. Conversely if a pivoting joint is required, such as in a pair of tongs, a round rivet should be set in the usual way, and the two pieces pivoted vigorously while the joint is still hot. This stretches and loosens the joint.

Riveting can be seen as a rather daunting and irreversible process. But if a rivet fails to give a tight joint, or if the two mating faces turn out to be misaligned, it is easy enough to drill out a rivet and start again. Centre punch the end of the rivet, as near the centre as possible, and drill right through, using a drill very slightly smaller than the rivet diameter. This leaves

Punched hole and riveted joint in a piece of 150mm (6in) square bar becomes a feature in this sculpture by Terry Clark.

the rivet as a thin shell that can be snapped and the fragments driven out.

Mortise and Tenon Joints

Mortise and tenon joints are in effect integral rivets. One component has a tail – the tenon – projecting from a shoulder that fits into a shaped hole in the other component – the mortise. The tenon is heated, inserted and riveted over, locking the two parts together. Tenons on square and round bar are usually circular in section and on flat bars they are usually rectangular.

Because the tenon needs to be accurately shaped from a shoulder, it is easier to make on a power hammer, or with the help of a striker. Top and bottom tools can be aligned and used more effectively. It is however quite possible to make tenons, working single handed, if stands are used to support the bar with its end located on the edge of the anvil or swage. A top tool can be held in one hand and a heavy hand hammer used to strike it.

A 'butcher', a special type of hot set with a flat face and a concave edge, is used to nick the corners of square bar all round,

to isolate the end of the tenon. With the cut located on a square edge of the anvil and a set hammer held above, the metal can be drawn down square, turning on the other face after every few blows. The initial necking may also be achieved using a 'side set', a type of set hammer with an angled face.

The square shank is finally rounded up in a top and bottom swage, starting the process by holding the bar with a corner uppermost and rounding the corners first. Before the tenon cools down, reheat it to the shoulder and fit a monkey tool over it, striking its end and rotating it to equalize any bending. The monkey tool upsets and squares the shoulder. The shoulder may be squared up to retain its original profile or considerably upset to provide a flared form at the end of the bar. If the bar is reasonably heavy, it can be laid horizontally over the edge of the anvil and its own weight will provide enough resistance when the monkey tool is hammered. With a short bar it may be better to rest its other end on the anvil face and drive the monkey tool straight down.

Detail of mortise and tenon joints and collars used through pairs of punched holes for the Treasury gates in Guildford Cathedral, by the author.

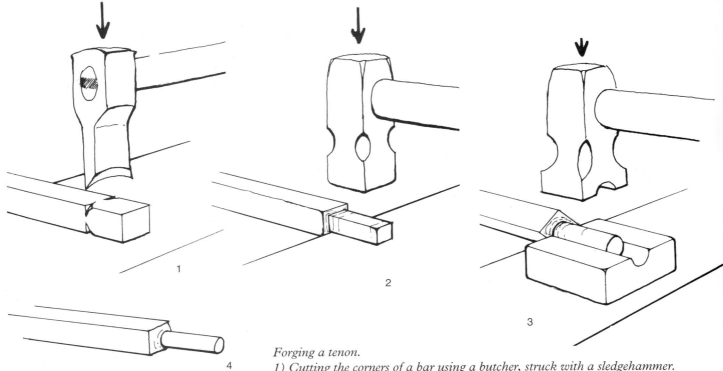

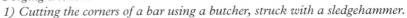

Forging a tenon.
1) Cutting the corners of a bar using a butcher, struck with a sledgehammer.
2) Forging a square tenon using a set hammer, struck with a sledgehammer.
3) Rounding the tenon in top and bottom swages.
4) The tenon swaged.
5) The shoulder of the tenon finished with a monkey tool.

ABOVE: Using a monkey tool to finish a tenon and upset the end of the bar.

ABOVE RIGHT: The finished tenon and monkey tool.

Monkey Tools

Monkey tools are needed for each size and shape of tenon. Tools for round tenons are easily made by drilling a blind hole centrally into the end of a suitable short piece of tool steel bar for perhaps two-thirds of its length.

Old road breaker bits annealed in the fire, can be cut with a square end to make good monkey tools. Most tools need only be around 100mm (4in) long. Just the end with the hole should be hardened. Some monkey tools are made with a large hole cut across the body so that the red hot tenon can be seen inside, and shortened before it contacts the blind end of the hole. The cross hole is not essential for this purpose, but there may be more value in drilling a hole simply to vent hot air and gas.

Tenons on flat bars are usually cut away with a chisel to leave the required size, then the ends rounded in swages and monkeyed to square the shoulder. These monkey tools can be made as described, but with rather more difficulty. A short row of holes must be drilled, plugged with mild steel, then more holes drilled in between. In this way a rectangular hole with rounded ends may be finished with a file.

Mortises

Mortises are provided by punched holes. Even if made with great care, one side of a punched hole usually looks better than the other. The edges tend to be dragged in a little by the punch. Choose the flattest side of the bar to receive the shoulder of the tenon. The less good side, where the edges of the hole have been pulled in, will be covered when the head of the tenon is riveted over.

Assemble the joint cold and carefully check the fit. It is the shoulder that controls the finished position of the two parts, so if necessary refine the fit with a file before riveting, to ensure that the joint seats correctly. The far end of the bar will need to be backed up to allow the tenon to be riveted. If possible, arrange the assembly vertically so that the end of the bar can be set on an anvil or a heavy block on the floor. If the tenon has to be riveted horizontally, a helper can back up with a heavy sledge or bar, or if all else fails a loose leg vice can be laid on the bar and clamped to it, to provide resistance.

COLLARS

Collars, also called 'clips', are a feature of much traditional ironwork, and are used in contemporary work. They can provide

valuable visual emphasis to a joint and convey a feeling of strength. A collar consists of a short piece of bar, usually flat in section, shaped to fit snugly around two or more other bars to connect them. They were often used to secure adjacent scrolls, where the two curves touched, or to hold scroll work to a frame.

The collar is bent and forged over a mandrel, opened up and slipped red hot over the bars to be secured. While still red hot the collar is closed with tongs, tapped with a hammer to tighten it and allowed to cool. 'Clip tongs' are required both to open out the collar and to clinch it in place. Fitted correctly the collar contracts as it cools and grips tightly. A creaking or ticking sound can often be heard as the contraction takes place and this is a good sign that the collar will hold tight.

Collar may have straight butted ends, be scarfed, or cut to an oblique angle, but the making process is very similar. Since the scarfed and oblique ends overlap, these collars are a little more forgiving to fit. If, as is normally the case, two bars of the same size are to be collared together, the mandrel can be made by doubling back the end of a handling length of this bar and tapping it carefully back on itself to make a 75mm (3in) length of double thickness. Forging the tip of the doubled bar to a short taper, just a little longer than the width of the collar, helps when the collar is to be removed. But take care not to distort the doubled section.

Making a collar.
1) A mandrel, representing the size of the two bars to be joined, made by doubling over a single bar.
2) The flat bar for the collar measured, part cut at the right length and bent to a 'U' shape.
3) The collar snapped off the bar, trapped over the mandrel and dressed down to shape.
4) A finished collar.
5) A collar reheated and opened up, ready for fitting.

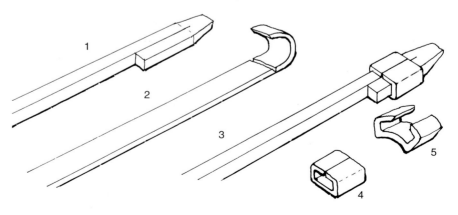

The length of metal needed to make a collar that will fit neatly around the mandrel is ultimately established by trial and error. But there are rules of thumb. With the mandrel laid at one end of the bar from which the collar is to be made, roll it along until all four faces have been measured out along the bar, then add twice the thickness of the material and make a chalk mark. Measure and note the length. Take a yellow heat, cut the length almost through over the hardie and bend it to a 'U' shape. Take another heat, fit the 'U' over the mandrel, snap it off the parent bar and hammer the 'U' around the mandrel, keeping it symmetrical and dressing the metal down neatly, so that the ends of the collar are centred on one long side of the mandrel. Preheating the mandrel a little will help prevent the collar from chilling too quickly. Speed is important or the collar can lock tight on the mandrel. Before it cools too much, locate the edge of the collar against the far edge of the anvil and strike the tapered end of the mandrel to drive off the collar, rotating it as it goes.

The usual practice is to make all the collars for a particular job, then reheat and fit them as a separate operation. Collars are notoriously easy to lose in a coal or coke fire, so thread them on a piece of thin rod to heat them up. At a bright red heat clip tongs can be used to pull open a collar, fit it over the joint and clinch it into place. In some situations, a hammer or a pair of hammers may be used to help fit the collar. Do not over-hammer the collar or you will loosen it. Set it quickly into place, tighten and leave it alone to cool.

The contraction of a hot collar means that it can provide a very strong mechanical

Sample piece for the Great Hall gates in Winchester, by Jim Horrobin. The design uses groups of bars collared together and collars through holes and square rings.

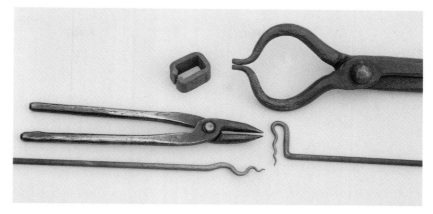

(Top) clip tongs used to open and close collars, together with a typical flat bar collar. (Bottom) round-nosed tongs used for manipulating thin bar, with typical bent details.

joint. But it may also make good sense to arc weld the metalwork first, then cover it with the collar. If the adjoining bars are bevelled with a grinder the weld can be placed in the recess. This may be needed in any case to hold the metalwork in place prior to collaring.

WRAPPING JOINTS

A wrapped joint is made by heating one piece of metal, usually round in section, and wrapping it around another, unheated piece, spiral fashion. The hot metal cools and contracts, gripping on to the other bar, to make a permanent joint. One bar may be wrapped over another to make a joint as described, or the wrap may be more like a collar. Two, or more, pieces are fitted side by side, and may be arc welded to each other, then a third piece wrapped around them. The finished effect is very much like a rope lashing.

Making structural wrapped joints has to a large extent been made possible by the use of the oxy-acetylene heating torch. Historically, the use of these joints seems to begin during the Art Nouveau period in Europe, at the very beginning of the twentieth century. It is, however, possible to make short wrapped joints by heating the wrapping piece in a fire and rapidly winding it around the other bar. But it is not so easy to create a reliable tight joint in this way. And if it goes wrong, it is even harder to remove, without the use of a torch.

Making wrapped joints in round bar, to make a bed head.

Wrapping absorbs surprising lengths of material. Since the circumference of a circle is 3.142 (π) $\times$ the diameter, it will need, for example, some 377mm (14¾in) of 10mm (⅜in) round rod simply to wrap four times around a single piece of 20mm (¾in) diameter. The required wrapping length can be calculated, remembering that it is the neutral axis (centre line) diameter of the wrapping bar that must be considered. A pragmatic answer is to use a piece of electric flex, plastic or rubber tubing of the same diameter wrapped around the joint the required number of times, unwound and measured. Knowing the length of the wrapping piece, arrange the workpiece in a vice with sufficient free space around so that the wrap can be pulled round without hitting obstructions. If necessary it can be doubled up, or even coiled to shorten its length.

Start the wrap by securing the end of the wrapping bar to the joint in some way. Make, for example, a short right-angle bend at one end of the wrapping piece and secure this to the joint in the starting position, using a locking wrench or other clamp; or tack weld it in a position that will be covered by the next rotation of the wrap; or a helper can clamp it with tongs. The length of wrapping bar can then be held in one hand and the gas torch in the other.

The wrap must always be heated at the bending point. If a little pressure is put on the wrap you will feel it give as the heat makes it plastic. Pull it immediately round the joint, keeping the torch always on the tangent point where it needs to bend. If the heating runs ahead of this point, the wrap will curl in the wrong place and may not seat down tight onto the bar. Play the torch on the wrapping piece and avoid heating the bar or bars underneath. Once a few turns have been established, the locking wrench can be removed and the wrap completed. If it becomes too short to hold, a piece of tube can be slipped over the end to provide leverage and the last turn tapped round with a hammer or mallet. If tails are going to be left, these can be adjusted and positioned afterwards, with a small pair of round-nosed tongs.

Wrapping round bar over round bar is simple and neat, but many other combinations are possible with a little care.

WEDGES, SPRINGS, PINS AND TABS

Collaring and wrapping exploit the contraction of the metal to tighten the joint. With a little ingenuity this property can be exploited in other ways. At the simplest, the appropriately sized hole can be drilled in a bar, the bar heated and a cold pin or bar driven through. The hot bar cools and contracts, locking the pin in place. It helps the pin enter the hole if it is slightly tapered at the end. A pin can be locked into a blind hole in the same way.

Fully tapered pins can also be driven in cold to make a fixing, and wedges can

ABOVE: The entrance to the Bar Estilo, Richmond, by Shelley Thomas, showing a decorative wrapped joint.

Detail of grandmother clock by the author, showing tapered pins driven through tenons, a traditional method of securing the back and front plate of a clock mechanism.

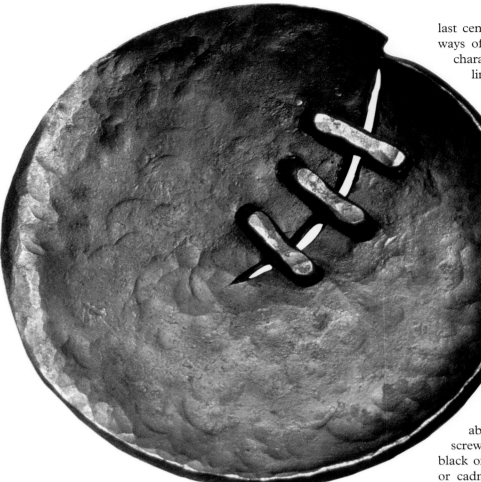

Forged steel bowl with stitches, by Jim Horrobin.

last century. Many smiths have developed ways of making joints that give a unique character to the piece of work. The only limit is your imagination.

NUTS, BOLTS AND SCREWS

Since these are fitted cold, all the components can be finished before assembly and the fixings are adjustable and removable. But the standard engineering product is often completely out of character with forged metalwork. Increasingly these fixings seem only to be available with a cadmium or zinc-plated finish, which provides corrosion protection but makes even small screws stand out as little silver spots against the black forged surface. If this is unacceptable, the plating can be burnt off steel screws at red heat, leaving them with a black oxide surface. (Avoid breathing zinc or cadmium fumes. Let them go up the forge chimney.) Dropping the hot screws into oil at black heat can improve the black finish. Bolt and screw fixings are available with a variety of head forms, some of which are more applicable than others. Hexagon socket heads, either cylindrical or countersunk can offer a less obtrusive detail, and usually have an oil blacked finish. Standard hexagon bolt heads can be hot forged to some other shape, but nuts usually need to be forged from scratch. Ball-shaped nuts are commercially available.

Screw threads are cut using taps and dies. The tap cuts a female (internal) thread, and the die cuts a male (external) thread. Appropriate wrenches are needed to hold taps and dies. Detailed information is available in books on engineering

similarly be arranged to provide connections. Wedges can be used to draw a joint tight and can provide a very expressive detail There is much to be gained by researching fixings. There are details used in other crafts and industries that repay study. Mortise and tenons joints would have been used in timber construction long before metalwork. Some wooden furniture uses a long tenon that comes out of the far side of the joint and is retained by a tapered peg driven through. Clockmakers used a similar detail to retain brass pillars and plates. Tabs can be bent through slots or around bars, to join one part to another, a device employed in the cheap tinplate toys made earlier in the machine-shop practice. But a few observations are worth making from a blacksmithing point of view.

There are a surprising number of different standard screw thread forms still in use. In your own workshop you can choose to use one type, and stick to it. Otherwise you will need a multitude of different taps and dies. ISO Metric coarse is the most generally applicable in Britain. Always buy high-speed steel (HSS) taps and dies. Carbon steel ones are a great deal cheaper but will dull rapidly when cutting mild steel and are ultimately a waste of money. High-speed steel tools can be bought individually as the need arises, so a set can be accumulated over a period of time. The same comments apply to drill bits.

Dies are intended for use on a precise diameter turned in a lathe, but with care, can be used satisfactorily on the appropriate diameter of stock bar, or round swaged section. Internal threads require a particular diameter hole to be drilled that is smaller than the finished thread size. This is called the tapping drill size. Some taps have this size etched on the shank, and tables of tapping drill sizes are printed in engineering handbooks. Taps are available in sets of three – taper, second and bottom taps. The taper tap has a long tapered lead, enabling the end to enter the hole made by the tapping drill. This must always be used first, to start the thread. The bottom tap has no taper and is threaded to the end enabling a blind hole to be threaded to the bottom. The second tap is optional.

Fixings are usually made by passing screws through clearance holes in one component to thread into holes in another. To lay out the pattern of holes, drill right through the top component first, but use the tapping drill. This part can then be used as a jig to drill the blind holes, by clamping both pieces together. The blind holes can then be tapped, and the through holes drilled out to the necessary clearance diameter, with both sets in perfect alignment.

BRAZING AND HARD SOLDERING

These processes may occasionally be needed in a blacksmithing workshop. Both use non-ferrous metals to form a joint between two pieces of steel or between steel and another metal. Brazing uses brass and hard soldering uses silver-based alloys. The surfaces to be joined need to be clean, bright and well-fitted. The joint is fluxed with a paste of borax and water and tiny scraps of solder are placed on the joint that is heated with a torch, fusing the flux. Solder may alternatively be fed directly onto the heated joint from a rod. When the solder melts it floods into the joint, carried by the capillary action of the flux, so that the internal surface is held by the solder. In this sense it is more like gluing than arc or gas welding, and because of the area involved, joints made in this way can be remarkably strong.

Demonstration piece made by Alan Evans. The structure is held together by cross bars passing under and over the uprights, secured by spring pressure.

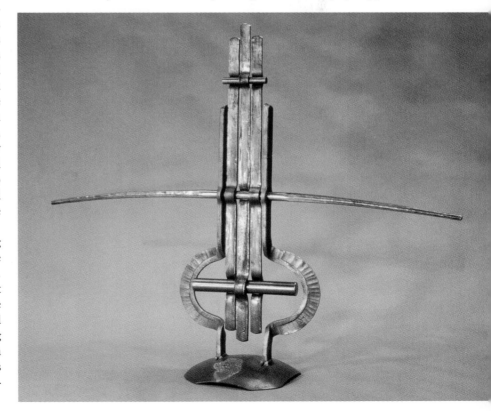

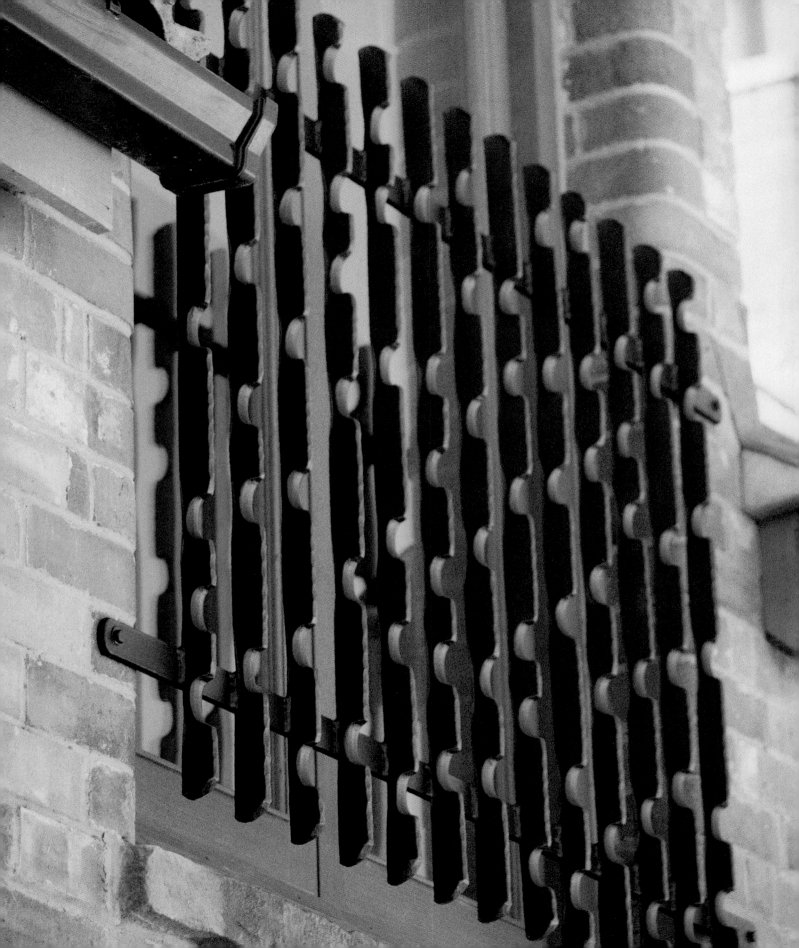

12 WORKING WITH A STRIKER

Many smiths work alone, but there are occasions when another pair of hands is necessary, if only to hold the other end of a long piece of metal. Traditionally a smith would have an assistant – a striker – whose job was to work at the other side of the anvil wielding a sledgehammer. Today the place of the striker is often taken by the power hammer. But while, as the saying has it, a power hammer doesn't answer back, there are still many forging operations that are better achieved with the help of a striker. He will not be as strong or as tireless as the power hammer, but his ability to respond to the needs of the job are clearly greater.

A power hammer can apply considerable force, but only in one direction. Just as blows from a hand hammer can be applied at any number of angles, so the sledge may be used to strike obliquely as well as providing the kind of vertical blows delivered by a power hammer. The striker may hit the metal directly, or he may strike the tools held by the smith. The smith holds the workpiece and the tool, while the striker provides the impact. The striker can also use his sledge to 'back up' hand hammering processes, for instance by holding his sledge on top of a bar while the smith bends it over the edge of the anvil, or using the hammer to provide resistance at one end of the bar while the smith rivets the other.

TECHNIQUE

The sledge is held much in the same way you would hold a hand hammer. That is to say, for a right-handed smith, by gripping

the middle of the shaft in the right hand. The left hand is then brought across the body to hold the end of the shaft. Striking in this way requires practice and may initially feel rather odd. But it has the great virtue that the striker swings the hammer straight down, just like a hand hammer, without at any time obscuring his view of the target. There is a tendency for beginners to hold the hammer shaft with their hands the other way round which results in a diagonal action, the hammer head starting from a position near the left shoulder and coming down at an angle across the body to strike a blow.

Using a sledgehammer is a potentially dangerous activity, and calls for concentration, trust and good communication between the smith and striker. Having several kilos of steel swung close to your head

Working with a striker, in Charles Normandale's workshop.

OPPOSITE PAGE: Window grille by Paul Margetts, illustrating the drama of repetition, achieved by fullering into the bar at irregular intervals.

focuses the mind wonderfully. It is important to agree signals that can be clearly understood. There is no room for ambiguity or second thoughts as the hammer comes down. The striker's role is not just muscle. He must be attentive, understand the process and anticipate the needs of the job, but he should do nothing unless directed by the smith.

The smith can signal the striker with his hand hammer. Traditionally when he needed the striker, he would call him by tapping repeatedly on the anvil face. The striker would immediately stop what he was doing, pick up his sledge and be ready at the anvil. The smith strikes the work with his hand hammer, the position and force of the blow indicating to the striker where and how heavily he should strike. Each time the smith makes a blow, the striker follows, until the smith hammers on the face of the anvil, which is the signal to stop. The speed, rhythm, power and placing of the blows are all controlled by the smith. In heavy industrial smithing, the smith might use a group of two or three strikers, working in sequence, to place multiple blows.

The direct hammering of the metal has become less commonplace, since power hammers now provide this function. But using a striker to drive punches, hot chisels, swages and other set tools is still a very useful and efficient way of working. If you work by yourself it is possible to use many of these tools under a power hammer, but working with a real human being is far more flexible.

Straight pein sledgehammer.

Since the smith holds both the workpiece and the set tool, he cannot signal with a hammer and has to shout commands. Simple words like 'yes' and 'no', or 'go' and 'stop' are probably best. Even then there needs to be a high level of non-verbal communication. The smith will, for example, position the head of the tool with a very deliberate gesture, then raise the handle until it is level, which indicates that it is ready to be struck. The striker must be well aware of the effect of each blow and draw on his experience to know how hard to strike.

There can be great satisfaction in working in this way. The smith is free to concentrate on positioning the workpiece and placing the tool accurately, while the striker can focus on providing a good solid blow. It can also be fascinating to watch people working together, who share such a high level of understanding.

Hammers

The pattern of sledgehammer commonly available in Britain is mainly intended for driving stakes into the ground or for breaking concrete. It has a long shaft and a relatively long octagonal section head, often with slightly domed faces. A shorter more compact head is desirable. Square-faced, cross-pein sledges are available that suit smithing purposes better. The shaft of a standard sledgehammer is often too long and needs shortening back, so that the end of the handle does not catch the striker's leg when he brings it down.

Cross-pein sledgehammer.

Dead weight helps to break concrete, but for blacksmithing, accuracy is more important. So choose a hammer that can be handled with comfort. A 10lb, or even a 7lb hammer striking reliably is far more use (and less frightening), than a 14lb hammer used erratically.

Working with a striker comes into its own in activities such as punching or hot cutting, or any process that requires top and bottom tools. Punching a hole through round bar is difficult when working by yourself, because the bar cannot simply be placed on the anvil and will rotate if hit slightly off-centre. You need three hands. Because the tool is placed precisely before it is struck, a set hammer can be used to forge an inside corner that could not be hit cleanly with a hand hammer; a flatter can be used to smooth a surface; top and bottom swages and fullers may be used in precise alignment, or a tenon may be forged between a set hammer and the edge of the anvil.

Entrance gates by Alan Evans. The decorative pattern of bends is achieved driving a fuller into the bar, supported over a swage.

13 DESIGN

Design is a large subject to deal with in a single chapter. It is the the matter of many complete books and the basis of countless Art College degree courses. But it is important to discuss it briefly here, because it has been the driving force behind the renaissance in blacksmithing in Britain and in many other countries. It is the development of new design ideas that has given rise to a contemporary blacksmithing movement.

Design is not, in my view, simply the province of people who are thought to be 'gifted', 'creative' or 'have flair'. It is significant that artists and designers refer to their activities as 'work'. Thomas Edison is quoted as saying that genius is one per cent inspiration and ninety-nine per cent perspiration. Behind most good works of art, or pieces of design, there is far more likely to be a great deal of sheer hard work, than simply the spontaneous output of a 'gifted' person.

LOOKING

Even if you do not think of yourself as creative, be prepared for some hard work and you could be surprised. A great deal of design thinking has to do with looking. We are taught from an early age to read words and to deal with figures, but not to look. That is to say looking, as distinct from seeing. In normal life we usually only bother to see things well enough to avoid tripping over them. We do not spend time looking critically and observing their form, detail and colour. But develop an interest in a particular field, and you will begin to see things far more perceptively.

If you have just bought a car, you will be far more likely to notice all the others of the same make. They were there all the time, but you just didn't notice them. Indeed, the real enthusiast will be capable of spotting a rare variation at an extraordinary distance. The dog owner will look at another dog of the same breed and see that its muzzle is a little short, its back is dipped and it is rather overweight. The non-dog owner will be far less discriminating, or may not even notice the dog. This is not a question of eyesight, but simply one of tuning in, becoming aware of particular shapes and forms and developing a sensitivity to them.

This only comes about through practice. You need to do a lot of press-ups to make your arms stronger, and you need to do a lot of serious looking to begin to develop some discrimination. So, tune in to metalwork. Study it. Look at metalwork in the street, visit shops, museums, and craft galleries and look at the metalwork there. If candleholders are your latest project, look at candleholders. But not simply metal ones, look also at the products of other crafts. Most of all look critically.

If you look critically, it ceases to be a passive activity. If you like what you see, analyse why you like it. Can you identify the qualities which make it appealing? Do not be inhibited by wondering whether you *should* like it. What do you honestly feel? If you don't like it, spend time considering why. What could be done to improve it? All these considerations are important.

Exercising your ability to make judgements is as crucial to the artist or designer as press-ups are to the gymnast. If you do not practise making critical, visual judgements at every possible opportunity – indeed as a matter of habit – you will perhaps exercise this faculty only a few times a year, when you design something of your own. And a few times a year is probably not enough.

DESIGN CONSIDERATIONS

Many distinct aspects go into the development of a good piece of design. Some can be identified by asking the right questions. What is this object for? Who is it for? What is it trying to say? What is its function? The function may be utilitarian or decorative or, more often, some combination of the two. If an object has a utilitarian purpose, it is important that it actually does work. A candleholder that can't hold candles is hardly good design, however beautiful it may be as a form. But this may be a question of degree. We are often prepared to compromise the utilitarian aspects somewhat, if it benefits the appearance.

A pair of forged steel hooks to fix your child's swing to the apple tree, clearly need to function with a good safety margin, while their appearance can take second place. (Although if they are made to function well they will, at the very least, have an appearance of honest utility). But the candleholder may perhaps be forgiven for dripping a little wax, if it looks better with a pan that is technically a fraction small.

There are invariably some guiding factors that need to be identified at the beginning of each new project. List the purposes, and establish the guiding dimensions. How tall should the candleholder be? Is it to stand on the floor or on a table ? What size candle is it intended to hold? Designing for a particular candle may provide a basis for new ideas. Candles are available in a huge variety of shapes and sizes, tall, thin, short and fat or even spherical. Check them out, don't assume the size of the candle. Bringing together this information begins to create a kind of skeleton of the design. Whatever the thing looks like, it will need to do this, hold a candle this size, be this tall and maybe this wide. A dimensional framework will begin to emerge.

Perhaps the most crucial question is – what if? What if I do design a candleholder around this odd little chunky candle? What if I think of as many ways as I can of simply holding a candle and stopping it falling over? What if I base the design on a particular plant form? What if I try to use this particular metal section? Could I make a candleholder just using one particular technique? What if I try to make a candleholder out of just one piece of metal?

And what about the character of the thing? Should it be slim and elegant, fine and delicate, chunky and solid, richly decorative, whimsical or just simple and well proportioned? And so on. Should it look heavy or light? The choice of materials can have a dramatic effect. A floor-standing candleholder made from 12mm round bar may look slim and delicate. But the same material used for a small table candleholder, may look very heavy. Which, of course, could be just the quality you are after, if the piece is intended to look solid and chunky.

DESIGN SOURCES

Designers tend to avoid the word 'inspiration', probably because it suggests that design is an instant, fully rounded thought that comes to mind like the illuminated light bulb over the cartoon character's head. But the notion of some kind of spark, a starting point or source, is nevertheless a valid one. A fully detailed design may not spring to mind instantly, but it has to start somewhere and a whole variety of thoughts and observations may provide that starting point. Many of the questions above could offer that initial spur.

ABOVE: What if? What if I use chain for part of the structure of a gate? A gate for a private house by Peter Crownshaw.

RIGHT: Wonderful plant imagery used in a gate by Avril Wilson for the entrance to the wildlife park in Southampton.

But designers will talk of 'sources' informing an idea. Meaning that some initial observation has given impetus to the thought. The impetus is not a random one but something the designer has sought out. It may be that the candleholder is intended for a particular room. In which case, sources – shapes, details, forms of construction, motifs and so on – may be found in the furniture, the decoration of the room or the architecture of the building itself. Or if the candleholder is for a particular person with an interest in, say, gardening, plant forms might be the source. Nature, and perhaps in particular plant forms, have been a perennial source for artists and designers throughout history. (And if the person is actually interested in motorbikes, embroidery or scuba diving, the principle remains the same.)

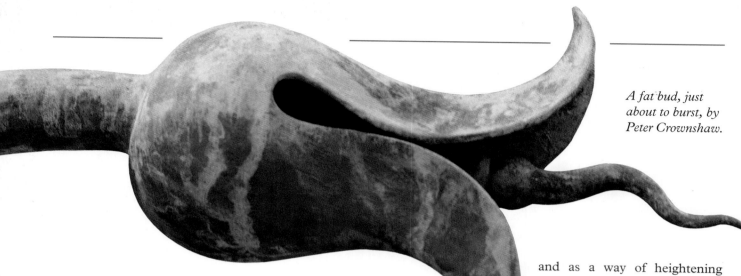

A fat bud, just about to burst, by Peter Crownshaw.

The important thing is to look at the source yourself. If you are making something using, for example, leaf shapes, go and look at real leaves, rather than looking at pictures of leaves. Collect them, draw them, photograph them, most of all make them *your* leaf shapes. Unless you go directly to sources, there is a danger that the image will be just a symbol. If your leaf is based on a forged leaf in a book that itself was probably based on another forged leaf, nothing has been gained and an opportunity has been lost. Eventually it becomes just a notional leaf. There is an immediacy and freshness that can only come from direct observation.

DRAWING

The traditional means of designing is through drawing. Using drawing not as an end in itself but as a means of recording, reviewing and developing ideas. The drawing is not a piece of art, to be hung on the wall, but visual notes made in preparation for making. And here perhaps is the biggest stumbling block. Many people profess to being unable to draw, and are inhibited from even trying. Yet many will cheerfully admit to having terrible handwriting, and it doesn't stop them doing it. As G.K. Chesterton said, if a thing is worth doing, it is worth doing badly. And it *is* worth doing.

Drawing is taught in Art Colleges both as an essential means of communication and as a way of heightening observation. Press-ups for the eyes. There is little doubt that you will notice more if you sit for twenty minutes and draw, for example a motorbike, rather than just sitting and looking at it for the same length of time. If you think of the activity as 'making a drawing' the pressure is on you to produce some kind of artwork, with a composition, style and beauty of its own. But if you think of this activity as simply 'gathering information', then the obligation is to record the structure and detail of the bike, the number of spokes in the wheels, the way the seat fits to the tank, the pattern of bolts on the gearbox and so on.

The beauty of the pencil marks on the paper are not so important. Either the bike has five spokes or it doesn't. If your sense of perspective is poor, or your rendering of a wheel is not perfectly round, does it matter ? If what you have drawn is your code for 'round', the record is correct as information. The content of Medieval drawings is not invalidated because their sense of perspective seems odd, and the stonemason building the wall is nearly as tall as the castle itself.

So absolutely any kind of drawing is better than no drawing. Persevere. Remember that the drawing is a means to an end. Keep drawings. They are a record of ideas and far more worth keeping than last year's diary. A sketchbook in which you can record thoughts is a resource worth

OPPOSITE PAGE: Gate for Brasenose College, by Terry Clark.

Emerging from one upright of the gate is the face of a man – the Brasenose nose. A neat, witty and subtle design detail (inset).

BRASENOSE COLLEGE

FREWIN ANNEXE

Horizontal sundial by Andrew Rowe at Pontardawe near Swansea, a historic steel-making area. The use of chain refers to the history of steel-making in the area while the leaves symbolize regrowth. By standing on the step, the viewer casts the shadow.

developing and worth keeping ready to hand. Draw ideas as soon as you have them. They are elusive things and easily forgotten or mislaid. Think of your sketchbook as a databank. Never rely on your memory to store that wonderful notion you had last week. It is the best way of having a conversation with yourself.

CONCEPT AND DESIGN

It can be helpful to consider the design of a particular object in two stages. First the concept, the general configuration. For example, a coffee table may be round, square, rectangular, hexagonal and so on. It might be supported on one central leg, three, four or even six legs. It may have no actual legs at all and be supported by extending the top surface down to the floor at each end. These are not 'designs', but basic concepts that can be reviewed and selected separately from a consideration of the proportion of the table, thickness of material, choice of fixings and so on.

The detailed design stage should begin once the basic concept has been established. In this way, you are less likely to sidetrack yourself from considering whether to use two rivets or three to fix the legs, into the sudden thought that perhaps the table could have six legs after all. Not, I hasten to add, that you can or should stop this happening. It is simply that with such an intuitive process, anything you can do to break down the problem into smaller and more manageable parts is worth trying.

It is important also to look at alternatives. Don't just settle for the first thing you can think of. This may, in the end, be the perfect answer but the only way to be sure, is to spend time considering other possibilities against which to test your first thoughts. Remember to ask yourself – what if? A successful idea may be well worth using again in a different form. Artists have built a career on the exploration of one particular theme.

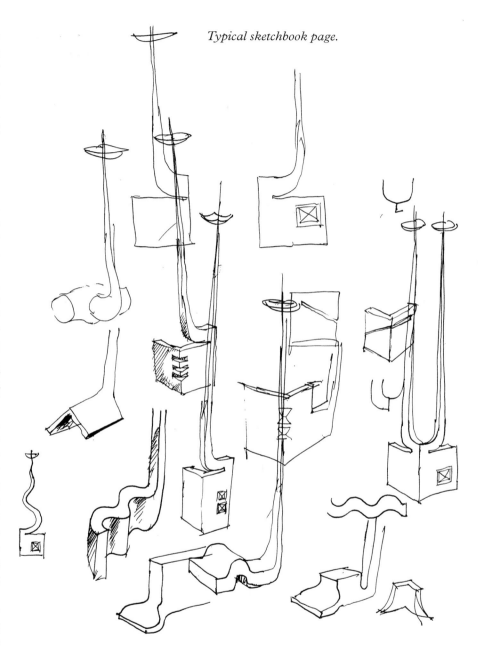

Typical sketchbook page.

ASPECTS OF DESIGN

Proportion

There are a number of important aesthetic considerations that must be touched on briefly. Proportion is a word that people may find intimidating, because it suggests the exercise of some rather refined and

Variations on a theme – Valentine tokens.

able to eliminate the extremes and arrive at a proportion you feel is right.

There really are no rules. Or rather there are some rules, but they should be taken with a good pinch of salt. The best known is the Golden Section, a mathematical ratio of 1:1.618 identified by Euclid. This describes the ratio of the lengths of the sides of a rectangle apparently preferred by a majority of people, and was used as a guiding ratio in classical architecture. Try it and see what you think. However, no matter how satisfactory this may be in some circumstances it is hard to see how one ratio could be universally applicable. (As a comparison, the familiar proportions of a sheet of A4 paper are 1:1.414.)

The traditional form of engineering and architectural drawing, using plans and elevations, is a very useful means of determining the sizes of components and how one part fits to another. But it is not such a good way of deciding how something will look. Drawn in elevation, 16mm round and square bar for instance, look the same. But in three dimensions round bar always looks thinner than square bar of the same size. Measured across the diagonal, square bars actually are something like 40 per cent larger than across the flats, and unrelieved flat surfaces always look larger than curved ones. So because of the way the light falls on the round section the discrepancy looks greater still.

Sometimes proportions within a construction may be altered by simple visual devices. The apparent width of square or flat bars can be reduced by bevelling the edges or cutting or fullering grooves along the bar to break up the flat face. Two thinner bars laid side by side will look thinner than one flat bar of the same width. Even laying a thinner bar over a wide flat bar can serve to reduce the apparent bulk.

elusive artistic judgement. But it describes nothing more than, say, the relationship between the length and the width of a table, or the size of one part in relation to another. The way to make this kind of decision is to try it, and see what you think. Test out the possibilities by drawing them to scale, or better still, drawing them full-size on a piece of board, or even the workshop floor. Once overall proportions have been decided, material sizes can often be established by laying pieces of bar on the full-size drawing. Indeed trying forged details or components on the drawing can be a good way of making many design judgements.

As a general principle it is a good idea to test ideas by taking them to extremes. A rectangular coffee table 90cm (3ft) long and 15cm (6in) wide is going to look very narrow, while 90cm long by 75cm (2ft 6in), may look too wide. But at what point in between does it just begin to look too narrow or too wide? In this way you will be

A gate in Salisbury Cathedral, showing the use of repeat pattern and illustrating the use of the visual devices of fullered grooves on the horizontal rail and applied bars on the vertical to reduce the apparent thickness of the bars.

Consistency of Detailing

Another important consideration is consistency of detailing. If one corner of the coffee table top is rounded, it seems logical that they should all be rounded. (Unless there is some very good reason not to.) All the parts of the object should look as if they belong together, and share some family resemblance. In practice this may mean limiting your choice of detail and process. It may be tempting to put together all your favourite ideas, motifs and details in one great tour de force. But however good they may look individually, there is no guarantee that they will sit very happily alongside each other, unless they share some kind of consistency.

Consider the whole design. Step back and judge it as a total object. Just as it is easy for the signwriter to misspell a word, because as he works he is only looking at the shape of a single letter, it is easy to be too close to your design and see only the details. The type designer has the problem of producing twenty-six components that may be used in almost any combination, but must always present a harmonious whole. Each letter must look as if it belongs to that particular alphabet family. If an odd letter seems to jump out of the word, the typographer has failed. And if an odd detail seems out of place in your design, think again.

This notion gives rise to the idea of a vocabulary of forms and details. Just as our language has changed, the vocabulary of forms used by blacksmiths two hundred years ago is (and should be) clearly different from the vocabulary in current use.

BELOW: Ministry of Health building at Richmond Terrace, Whitehall, London. The gate, designed by Jim Horrobin, is situated to the right of the main door.

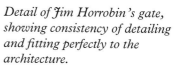

Detail of Jim Horrobin's gate, showing consistency of detailing and fitting perfectly to the architecture.

Contrast

Contrast is an important consideration. At first sight this might seem to be the opposite of consistency. But detailing can show consistency even though the components are of contrasting sizes. The tiny thin end to the long taper makes the thicker parts of the structure more dramatic by contrast (*see* page 43). The fine bar next to the thick one, or the little group of rivets against a large unrelieved surface, act as a foil to each other. Contrast in size, spacing and density of components can all contribute to a more exciting design. If consistency is slavish, it can lead to uniformity. Contrast can add a spark to the design.

Stereotypes

Our eyes are remarkably sensitive to a number of stereotypes. These include a horizontal line, a vertical line, a straight line, a circle, a square and a right-angle. Some people are, for example, intensely irritated by a picture hanging very slightly askew on the wall. It follows that if a piece of work involves any of these stereotypes, it had better be right. A slightly lumpy circle, a right-angle that is really 89 degrees or a rectangle that is very nearly a square will look uncomfortable, even if the viewer cannot explain why. If your design involves a horizontal line, a square, circle and so on, make sure they are true. And, if they are not supposed to be horizontal, square or whatever, make sure that they are sufficiently different not to look like a mistake.

Symmetry and Asymmetry

Symmetry is another familiar quality. If a centreline is drawn through the object, the form on one side of the line is mirrored on the other. One side balances and supports the other. If symmetry is the objective, then it is important that the piece be truly

'Four winds' pedestrian screens, Tower Place, Edinburgh, by Phil Johnson. They are powerfully symmetrical, centre pivoted gates that are redolent of square-rigged ships and the sea, just a little way off behind the wall.

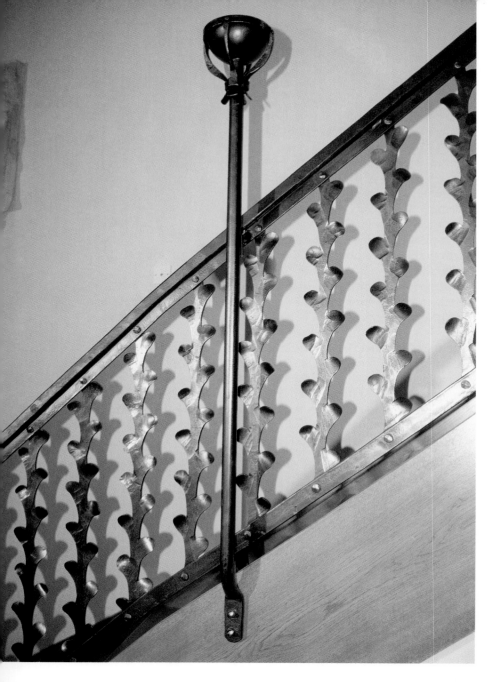

Repeat units making a balustrade by Charles Normandale. Each unit is laser cut then forged, the forging providing some variety within the design, that also meets the British Building Regulation requirement that a 100mm (4in) ball should not be able to pass through.

as a design tool to examine other sources such as magazine illustrations, letter forms, found objects like plants and twigs, and so on. Setting the edge of the mirror on the source material and dragging it across, will produce symmetrical patterns and can generate unexpected ideas.

Yet some departure from true symmetry can look exciting. Historically designers have played with the idea of symmetry by introducing some unexpected and asymmetrical element into a design that at first sight seems to be truly symmetrical. A further step from this is the truly asymmetrical design. This can look less formal, less tranquil but more dynamic. An asymmetrical design also needs to balance, to suggest some sense of equilibrium. This may be harder to achieve but can offer a freer and more informal result. This kind of balance requires critical judgement. Turn the object round and look at it from all angles. A pleasing appearance from one viewpoint may not be so satisfactory when seen from another.

Repetition

Repetition can be a powerful factor in the design of gates, grilles and screens. Much traditional ironwork was based on the use of repeat elements, in the same way that textile designs employ repeated units. Indeed the patterns used in ironwork from the seventeenth to the nineteenth centuries, bear close comparison to contemporary textiles and wallpaper.

I have a book published in 1907 entitled 'Design for Schools', that is a handbook for teachers and very largely uses the word 'design' to mean a repeated flat pattern. Children were taught to draw from nature and use plant images to produce repeating patterns, not so much in preparation for careers as textile designers but as a means of developing observation, discipline and skills in drawing, brushwork and geometry.

The basis for much of this work is the use of grids as a format on which to overlay

symmetrical. Symmetrical designs tend to have a self-contained quality that can give them a certain authority. A good example is the paired entrance gates to a house, where the symmetry is only apparent when the gates are closed.

In preparing such designs, only half needs be drawn initially. A mirror held upright on the drawing will very quickly allow you to assess the overall appearance of the design. The mirror can also be used

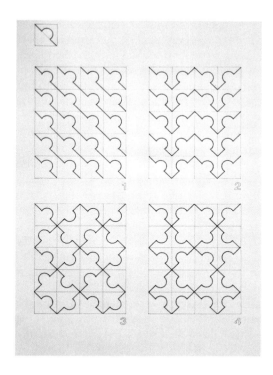

An example of designing repeat patterns on a grid. The basic unit is shown at top left, and the pattern areas show seven different possible arrangements of that unit. The patterns are arrived at by considering all possible permutations, arranging in lines, mirroring left to right, up and down, and rotating about a point. This strategy can be used to explore the pattern possibilities of any basic unit.

particular design motifs and examine their potential. For architectural metalwork, the power of repetition lies in the decorative value of the spaces between the metal elements as well as the elements themselves. Very simple design elements or motifs can become interesting through repetition. The whole becomes more than the sum of the parts. The technique of developing a repeat pattern by manipulating a simple motif on a grid can be an interesting and worthwhile exercise.

The Material

The material itself is a source of ideas. The metal is not just 'stuff', without intrinsic character, waiting to be forced into any form we desire. There are qualities it possesses and forged forms that seem eloquent of the material itself. There are 'metal' shapes and there are 'wood' shapes. It is the eternal problem of every craftsman to seek out and try to use those forms, details and qualities. The forged leaf, for example, should not be simply a

Four possible metalwork interpretations of pattern 4.

model leaf made in metal. As a successful piece of design it should say as much about the material as it does about the leaf.

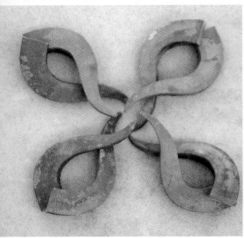

ends together to make a tight 'U' shape, the inside of the bend will be compressed upset sideways, while the outside of the bend will be stretched and narrowed. If you have in mind a geometric 'U' shape, you will immediately reach for the hammer and flatten the side of the bend to give it a 'proper' shape.

On the other hand, if you look at what has happened you will see a bend that also expresses the plasticity of the metal – not a 'perfect' bend but something more interesting. Do not be too hasty to 'correct' the metal. Forms and details can occur on the way to making the idea you have in mind, that may form the basis for new possibilities. Some of the quality of forging resides in the viewer appreciating the transformation that has taken place. If forging is all about moving metal, it is important to know what it has moved from. The short section of twisted bar is the more dramatic for being part of a length that is plain.

Experiment with the material. Asking yourself 'what if?', applies as much in the workshop as in the sketchbook. Playing with the components of a piece of work before you finally assemble them is almost always worthwhile. Try them in different arrangements and take photographs. This can generate a number of new ideas in a very short space of time.

COMPLETING THE DESIGN

An experiment may lead directly to the design of a new piece of work, the design evolving in the workshop. Others may need drawings, measurements, test pieces and more drawings before reaching a conclusion.

Depending on the nature of the project, you may be able to make the metalwork from a scale drawing. If a gate or screen is an assembly of bars within a frame, components can be made to the dimensions on the drawing and assembled on trestles (*see* page 19).

Asking a what if question by playing with forged parts before they are assembled for their proper purpose. These formed the front of a fire-grate.

Forging exploits the plasticity of the metal and familiarity with forging processes leads to the idea that the metal 'wants' to take on particular forms. Being sensitive to the way it moves and observing the result can be a source of design ideas. If, for instance, you take a very short, yellow heat in the middle of a piece of 12mm (½in) square bar and pull the two

The material itself can be a source of ideas. Detail of work in forged bar and tube in the Bar Estilo, by Shelley Thomas.

For other items, a workshop layout drawing may be necessary. This can be as simple as a few lines chalked on the floor, showing the overall size and shape of the item. Or it may need to be a detailed, full-size elevation drawing on a suitable flat surface. In general, if it is important to make something accurately to dimensions – a staircase balustrade to fit a particular space in a building for example – an accurate layout drawing is likely to be needed. But this is always a matter of judgement, since making the drawing can take some time. On balance it is often better to make a drawing, since it enables construction problems to be anticipated and, at the very least, allows you to visualize the object full size.

Each component can then be made and laid on the board. Small engineer's squares stood upright on the drawing can be used to to check its shape. The whole assembly may indeed be put together on the board. Large pieces of blockboard or MDF make good layout boards. These can be laid on trestles, painted with a light-coloured emulsion paint and drawn on with pencil, using a T-square against one edge. The board can be painted over again for the next project. If it is likely that the metal will be hot when placed on the board – when, for example, bending a bar to a particular curve – it is better to use a piece of steel plate as the layout board, or at least to lay out that particular curved component. Old rusty plate takes a chalk line more clearly than the mill scale surface of new plate.

Finally, whatever approach you use, do not be too constrained by your drawing. If, once you have the component in your hand, it seems better to make it rather differently, do so. There is no virtue in reproducing, for example, the curve on the drawing if the curve you have just made looks better.

14 JIGS AND TOOLS

orging a single item can be achieved with freedom and spontaneity. But it can be a different problem to produce a number. A piece of work – perhaps a gate or screen – might require several identical units within it, or an item originally made as a one-off piece may prove so successful that the need arises to reproduce a number of similar items.

It is relatively easy, for example, to produce tapers of the same length, or spread metal to the same width each time. A rule or a pair of callipers are an easy means of ensuring that the sizes are the same. But if the component is curved or bent, some other way must be found to ensure that each piece has the same curve. The simplest approach might be to lay one piece on top of the other. One piece can be kept to one side as a master and all others compared with it. Placing one piece over the other and eyeing them up is of limited accuracy. It is more revealing to set the master level on a flat surface, lay the new component on top and use a square, or several squares, to check the profile.

OPPOSITE PAGE: Part of a length of railing at Penrith, by Brian Russell. Several jigs were needed to bend each unit. An example of the richness of pattern generated by repeat units. The tiny 'bud' emerging from the paving between each unit is there to fill the space, in order to meet the British Building Regulation that to protect a drop, a 100mm (4in) diameter ball should not be able to pass through the bars.

For some purposes, this may be sufficient, but it is a matter of judgement whether it will be quicker in the long run to spend time making some more sophisticated aid. The decision is a balance of time saved, numbers required and the degree of accuracy necessary.

TEMPLATES

Rather than compare one item directly with another, it may be more expedient to make some form of pattern or template. These are usually made of thin sheet metal and take the form of a gauge to check the profile of a shape. The metal is forged, checked with the template and adjusted until it is

Sheet metal templates, for various radii, curves, a small coal shovel and, at the centre, a pattern for the bracket used in the gate shown on page 127.

correct. The template may be the same shape as the required item, or a negative shape, enabling it to fit against the test item. In general, a template is more accurate if it can fit directly against the edge it is checking. Templates may also contain information such as the position of holes, to be marked through with a centre punch, rather than measuring and setting out separately on each component. A template may be as simple as a semi-circle of sheet metal, to check a bend radius, or as large and complicated as a timber and hardboard construction used to reproduce the profile of an arched stone gateway.

Sheet metal templates are a useful way of storing information. The form of a blank to forge a ladle or small shovel is a good example. It takes time and perhaps some experimentation to arrive at these profiles in the first place, so it makes sense to keep the results for future reference. Drilling a hole through the template and hanging it on a nail is an easy way to store it.

JIGS AND TOOLS

The engineering definition of a jig is a device that holds the work and guides the tool, while the tool does the work. But with many blacksmithing processes this distinction becomes rather blurred. A jig may be a tool. The most often needed are jigs that enable a particular curve or bend to be reproduced. These may be considered as templates thick enough not just to check the shape of the metal but to enable the hot metal to be bent over them.

BENDING TOOLS

Mandrels

A very simple jig is a mandrel, a length of steel bar held in the vice while a thinner bar is wrapped around it. Very thin rod – 6mm diameter or less – may be wrapped cold and will spring away from the mandrel when the tension is released, making a

larger diameter. Most wrapping is far easier using a torch to heat the metal. The workpiece is wound round in a tight spiral, then driven off the mandrel, using a hammer and a short piece of bar as a punch. Since the hot bar will cool and shrink onto the mandrel, this is easier while the spiral is still hot. It can also help to rotate it in the opposite direction to the wrapping.

The finished spiral may itself be the required item, or it may be cut with a hacksaw, or a thin cutting disc in an angle grinder, to produce a series of identical rings. The ends of each ring will be out of line by the thickness of the material and only need a slight twist in a vice to line them up. Since the shape of the ring depends on the profile of the mandrel, rings of a variety of shapes – round, square, oval, and so on – can all be made in this way. They can similarly be made in round and square bar, and even in flat bar if it is not too wide. If the intention is to make rings, it can be easier to take them off by cutting the spiral while it is still on the mandrel.

OPPOSITE PAGE: Large timber and hardboard template, made on site, to establish the profile of a stone arched doorway to a church.

BELOW: Detail of the gate, by the author made from the template (opposite). The gate incorporates stainless steel mesh to allow air into an unheated building, but fits tightly to the arch to keep out birds.

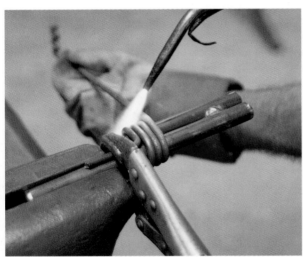

*THE MAKING OF OVAL RINGS
OVER A MANDREL.*

TOP LEFT: *Two bars tacked together to make
an oval mandrel, and the wrapping rod
secured with a locking wrench.*

TOP RIGHT: *The rod heated with a torch and
the first turn completed.*

MIDDLE LEFT: *Wrapping the rest of the bar.*

MIDDLE RIGHT: *Slitting the windings with a
1mm-thick cutting disc.*

LEFT: *Separate rings taken off. They only
need a slight twist in a vice to line up the
ends.*

TOP: *Using a mandrel, chalk marked to lay out an open spiral. The end is being bent with a scroll wrench, to place it on the centre line of the spiral.*

ABOVE: *The completed open spiral.*

An open spiral, can also be produced in the same way, by spacing out the turns. Wrapping a piece of plastic-coated washing line or flex over the mandrel enables the spiral to be set out and the line marked with chalk. The chalk line can then be followed with the hot bar. The mandrel can also be tapered, to produce tapered spirals. For many purposes, tapered mandrels can be forged accurately enough, but they may need to be turned in a lathe, or made from some object salvaged from a scrapyard.

Detail of flower stands by the author in Guildford Cathedral. Open conical spirals used to locate copper vases. The small flat spiral is a clip, used to hold a dedication card.

A magnificent radiator, by Lawrence Walker. Made by forged bar, and tube wrapped into a huge spiral coil.

Tools to Bend Rings

Tools to bend rings may be made by the smith, or adapted from found objects rescued from the scrapyard. Short ends of heavy steel tube, vehicle brake drums and odd nameless machine components can all make useful bending formers. Whether found, adapted, or workshop-made, bending formers need to be held solidly to withstand the leverage applied during bending. Pulling on a length of red hot metal at waist level and having the tool suddenly slip is a hazard. So bending tools need to be locked securely in a vice, or fitted with a shank to suit the hardie hole or a hole in a swage block.

Pieces of thick wall tube and other hollow forms make the best formers. They are better than solid ends of round bar, because one leg of the bending tool can locate inside the former. Thus the bar being bent can be secured around the profile using scroll wrenches, clamps or tongs, as bending proceeds. To adapt a found object, it may only be necessary to weld or bolt on a shank to fit the hardie hole, or be clamped in a vice. More tools can be generated from those you already have, by wrapping successive rings over each other.

Just as when making a ring over the bick of the anvil, it is better to determine the length required and bend the ends first. Each end of the bar should be dressed down neatly onto the former with a hammer, for a sufficient length to enable it to be clamped. The remaining hot bar can then be pulled round with a scroll wrench, one leg of which can be placed inside the former to give leverage.

When heating the bar in a forge, it will need several heats to complete the ring. If you wrap the hot bar round the former from one end, it becomes very difficult to

ABOVE: Using a ring bending jig. Dressing down the end of the bar to start the ring with the jig located in the hardie hole.

ABOVE RIGHT: Locking the end of the bar with a scroll wrench while pulling round the other end by hand.

USING A SPIRAL BENDING TOOL.
This is similar in form to a scroll bending tool.
BELOW: The tip of the workpiece has been started over the anvil so that it will hook over the centre of the tool.

BOTTOM: The first turn completed.

remove it to take another heat, when more than half the circle is complete. Pulling it round just short of half way from each end, then completing the circle with one heat in the middle is easier and quicker.

With a suitable gas heating torch, you will still need to dress down one end of the bar to begin, but you have the option of pulling the bar right the way round, heating as you go and dressing down the other end to complete the ring. As bending proceeds, the heat must always be applied at the tangent point where bending is taking place, or kinks will develop.

Tools to Bend Scrolls and Spirals

The tool itself is made from substantially thicker bar than the material to be bent, and one face is shaped to provide a curve corresponding to the shape required. If the bend is convex throughout, the outer edge of the jig is the required profile, and the hot workpiece is secured at one end and pulled around it, either by hand or using

USING A SPIRAL BENDING TOOL.

TOP: *The growing spiral is dropped lower down in the tool to engage with the lower turns.*

MIDDLE: *The completed spiral removed.*

BOTTOM: *A group of spirals all made on this tool. They were used as clips for the flower stand shown on page 129.*

bending wrenches. Tools to bend scrolls and spirals have the virtue that the constantly changing curvature helps to secure the hot bar to the jig without additional clamping, and similarly enables it to release cleanly when complete.

A classic example of this kind of jig is the scroll tool. The workpiece needs an initial tight bend made over the edge of the anvil to provide a little curve to locate the metal at the centre of the scroll tool, where it can be held momentarily with round-nose tongs. The bar is started by pulling it around the upper part of the tool using a scroll wrench, then dropped lower down to be pulled round the second turn. 'C' and 'S' scrolls can usually be made on the same jig.

The upstand – or offset – at the centre of the tool is an important feature enabling the workpiece to be pulled round more than 360 degrees. This principle can be applied to the making of a tool to produce any similar spiral form. To make the tool, use a flat bar that is thicker than the scroll to be produced and spread the end into a fairly wide fishtail. The fishtail is then offset to one side, to make one edge of the bar straight. The fishtail end should be cut or ground so that it is truly square to the straight edge, then the bar forged so that the outer face follows the required spiral curve, keeping the straight (bottom) edge of the bar in one plane. The line of the scroll should be carefully chalked onto a piece of steel plate and the tool forged accurately to fit it. Traditionally the 'tail' of a scroll tool is bent down at a right-angle, so that it can be wedged into the hardie hole or clamped in a vice.

Other Bending Tools

A multitude of other special bending tools may be made using the principles already described. These are that the accuracy resides in one working face, provision must be made for clamping and leverage, and there must be some means of removing the workpiece without jamming. Since

Using a bending jig made to give a specific angle.

Making short curves on the end of a bar using a jig. Note the chalk mark to locate the end of the bar.

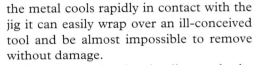

A simple bending tool, tacked together from odd scraps. The cylindrical pin determines the bend radius. The bar at the left provides a rigid fence, and can be chalk marked at different points to give different lengths of bend.

A similar bending tool, but the centre pin is bolted through a slot, to allow the centre pin to be changed. Two other centre pins are shown.

the metal cools rapidly in contact with the jig it can easily wrap over an ill-conceived tool and be almost impossible to remove without damage.

With the tools already discussed, the workpiece is bent in one direction. Complications can occur if the bar needs to be bent first one way, then the other. The process of bending the workpiece at one point may foul the tool at another. To overcome this problem the tool can incorporate loose, removable pieces. The hot workpiece is inserted and bent one way, a loose piece fitted to the tool and the bar bent back over it. There can, if necessary, be several loose pieces.

Bending jig with removable pieces that are pins located in holes.
1) The jig in use, showing one loose pin removed
2) Plan of the jig showing how the bar is inserted, the bar bent and pins inserted in sequence as bending proceeds.

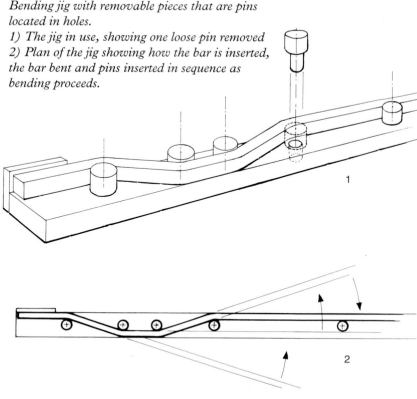

DRILL JIGS

Mention has been made of the use of templates to mark out holes. It is only a short step from this to a jig that locates the workpiece, or locates over the workpiece, and allows holes to be drilled without prior marking or centre punching. At the simplest, this can be a piece of plate, carefully marked out and drilled with the necessary holes, with fences, pins or brackets to locate it correctly against each workpiece and allow it to be clamped in place. Holes can then be drilled through, the same pattern being produced each time. A more sophisticated version might be made using carbon steel plate (vehicle leaf spring) that can be hardened, or using small hardened steel bushes fitted to each hole. These refinements are only worth considering if wear at the drill holes is likely to be a problem, which probably implies the making of several hundred units.

WELDING JIGS

These are devices to locate and hold components while they are gas or arc welded. Ninety degree and adjustable magnetic clamps are available commercially and can solve a lot of awkward problems. Since each case is different, it is hard to offer suggestions beyond a few general points. 'Over centre' or 'toggle' clamps are available from engineering suppliers, and are quick to lock and release. They can be bolted to a jig made of steel bar, to provide the required clamping.

A little thought is necessary to determine whether the jig simply needs to hold pieces in alignment or whether it will be subject to stresses set up by the welding itself. Weld metal contracts rapidly on cooling and pulls the metal in the direction of the weld, so unless the welding itself is balanced carefully, the jig may need to resist this contraction to maintain, for example, a right-angled corner. In this case, both the structure of the jig and the clamping will need to be substantial enough to resist movement. There are excellent welding handbooks dealing with the subject in detail.

If a large number of items are to be produced, it may be worth making a jig that locates and holds the whole item together, so that all the joints can be welded in one session. At the other extreme a very simple and universally adjustable holding mechanism is a bucket or tray of damp, soft sand. If the sand is rammed firm, awkward components may be pushed into it to hold them in place while they are welded.

HAND FORGING TOOLS

There are many blacksmithing tools that can be produced in the forge. The simplest are hand-held chisels and punches that can be made from suitable tool steel bar, salvaged material such as vehicle half shafts or torsion bars, truck coil springs or even old cold chisels. All of these are carbon steels. Coil springs or other salvaged material should be straightened out at a good red heat, and left to cool without quenching, which will serve to anneal the metal.

Forging carbon steel is straightforward but harder work than forging mild steel. Hot chisels should be drawn to a good thin edge, while cold chisels should be left thicker. A short taper should be forged on the end to be struck, to counteract mushrooming. The cutting edge and faces may then be ground essentially to the finished form. Punches can be forged to shape, allowed to cool slowly, then the tip ground and filed to a finished form. The tool now needs to be hardened and tempered. Even today this subject seems to speak of ancient mysteries and there is indeed something very intriguing in being able to shape metal, then harden it to provide a punch, cutting edge or spring.

Hardening and Tempering

If the end of a length of carbon steel bar is heated to red heat and rapidly cooled it will become hard. So hard that a file will slide across it without cutting and it will snap like a carrot when struck with a hammer. This state is called 'dead hard'. Tempering is the process of reducing this hardness and increasing the toughness to the required degree, by reheating to a particular temperature. The reheating is well below red heat so there is no radiant heat colour to indicate the temperature. But if the metal surface is clean and bright, oxide colours will form on the surface and these are a good indicator of temperature. They are produced by a very thin film of iron oxide – an interference film – similar in colour and effect to a film of oil on water. At different temperatures the film thickness varies and shows a different colour.

Temper Colours

The first perceptible colour is a pale straw. This reduces hardness the least, leaves the steel very hard and still a little brittle. It is used for tools that are not subject to impact, like scrapers and hand engraving tools. At a higher temperature, the straw becomes brown then purple then blue and finally grey. Tools subject to impact should tend towards the purple end. Beyond this, the blue colour is needed for springs. Tables are published in engineering handbooks suggesting particular colours for particular tools, but it should be emphasized that they are only a guide. The type of steel used will have a major part to play in the effectiveness of the tool, as will its thickness, so it is important to experiment so as to become familiar with the character of the particular steel you are using and the needs of the tool you are making.

Since the colour indicates the temperature of the surface of the metal, some care must be taken to ensure that the hardened tool has been heated right through. If a gas torch is simply played on the metal it can raise the surface temperature, showing heat colours, without necessarily penetrating the thickness of the tool. It is more reliable to allow heat to be conducted through the metal until the temper colour appears at the required place. There are two basic ways of doing this.

Tempering

The most instructive way is to use a hot piece of bar to draw the temper. Take the cutting end of the newly forged chisel to a red heat, for about a third of its length then quench the whole tool, agitating it in the water. Place a short, heavy piece of bar in the forge to heat. This can be much the same length as the chisel but thicker. It simply needs to be big enough to supply tempering heat to the chisel. Clean the end of the chisel – that is now dead hard – with an old grinder disc, or coarse emery paper, until it has one bright side for about half its length.

At dull red heat, take the bar from the fire and place it on the coal or coke, or on a firebrick. Lay the chisel on the hot bar, with the cutting edge projecting for perhaps a third of the length of the chisel and the bright side uppermost. The body of the chisel will now be heated and the heat will conduct along it towards the cutting edge, as it overhangs the bar. This takes place quite slowly and the colours can be observed travelling along towards the tip. As soon as the edge reaches a brown colour, pick up the chisel and quench the whole tool to stop the end overheating. This is a good way to temper chisels, punches and other small tools. A batch of tools can be forged, hardened, placed on the hot bar, picked off and quenched as they reach temperature. However it is important to note that tools should not be hardened and left too long before tempering. Internal stresses can cause the steel to crack if not relieved within an hour or so.

The second method applies to larger tools that can be tempered by using the residual heat left in the shank. The tool is heated to red heat for perhaps two-thirds of its length and just the cutting end quenched for about a third of the length, agitating the tool so that the cooling does not leave a sharp line, or the tool may crack at this point. This will leave the chisel with the cutting end dead hard and the middle still red hot. Holding it in tongs, brighten one side quickly with an old grinder disc and watch as the heat in the shank reheats the quenched end. When the required temper colour reaches the cutting edge, quench the end to prevent overheating. With practice this can be achieved at a point when the red heat in the shank has faded to black. If this is the case the whole tool can then be quenched, to prevent the tip overheating.

If the shank is still showing a heat colour, brighten the cutting end with the grinder disc, watch the colours, and if necessary quench again at the right colour. The crucial thing is to avoid quenching the shank end of the tool while it is red hot and causing it to harden. The part of the tool to be struck with a hammer should be left in an annealed state.

Quenching

Some steels are intended to be hardened by quenching in water, others in oil. This is a function of the carbon and alloy content of the steel and its thickness. Water provides a rapid quench, while oil is slower, so if a steel cracks in water, try it in oil. Used car engine oil smells terrible, but works. Thin sections are more likely to crack and need oil quenching. The oil should be in a metal container with a lid that can be dropped into place to kill the fire if the oil ignites. Very thick and compact steel sections may be better quenched with running water from a tap or a watering can. The face of a hammer or an anvil tool, for example, may need to be quenched in this way, pouring the water until it just wets the surface of the metal and using the residual heat to draw temper.

Once the tools are hardened and tempered, be aware that any subsequent reheating can kill the temper. Care must be taken when sharpening chisels against a grinding wheel. If temper colours appear on the ground edge, you are overheating it. Hot chisels should similarly be quenched frequently in use.

Case Hardening

Some tools may be made from mild steel and case-hardened. The purpose is to create a thin hard steel skin to the metal, while the interior remains soft. Traditionally this involves packing the items in a sealed iron box or 'case', surrounded by carbon in some form. The whole box is heated to red heat, and held at that temperature for a time. The soft steel absorbs some of the carbon, giving it a carbon steel surface. Commercial compounds are available to achieve a similar effect without need for the box.

The tool is taken from the fire at red heat and dipped in the case-hardening powder that fuses to the surface. It is then returned to the fire, held at red heat for a while and quenched in water. This can be a good treatment for tools that take pressure rather than impact, like the bottom tool that holds the head of a rivet or anvil swages.

SET TOOLS

With the help of a striker, tools with handles, such as hammers, chisels, punches and and fullers can be made essentially in the same way. The first stage is to drive a hole through the tool steel bar, using a sharp set chisel driven in from both sides. The hole is then drifted out with an oval drift, using it alternately from each side, to leave a neck in the hole.

For a hammer, the end of the bar can be forged to provide the required shape, the bar cut all round with a hot set to sever it and the cut end forged and ground to shape. The working ends of chisels, punches and fullers are best forged on the end of the bar, then the tool cut off and the top end forged and ground to shape. The hardest part of the process is cutting and drifting a neat hole, so salvaging hammer heads from car boot sales can be well worthwhile, to convert them into other tools.

ANVIL TOOLS

For anvil tools, start by forging the square shank that fits the hardie hole. Use a piece of bar of a section large enough to provide the body of the tool, fuller it all round, then draw down the shank from the fullered groove, over the edge of the anvil, using a set hammer and flatten. The shank should be tapered a little at the end so that its tip will enter the hardie hole, and the whole length driven into the hole at a yellow heat to finish it and seat the shoulder. The tool can then be cut from the bar and its working end forged and ground to shape. For swages, the body of the tool can be upset to a greater width as it sits in the hardie hole, and a piece of the required bar section laid across the face and driven in to create a groove. For fullers the tool is drawn down and ground to the finished form.

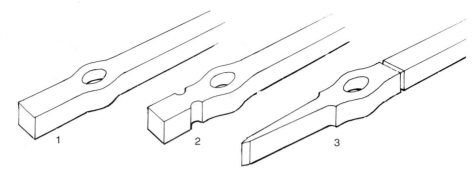

Forging a set chisel.
1) Punch and drift an oval eye for the timber handle.
2) Fuller just below the eye.
3) Draw down the chisel from the fullering. Cut off the bar, harden and temper the cutting edge.

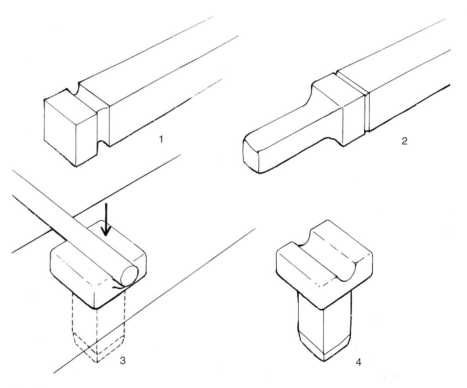

Forging a swage.
1) Fuller all round the bar.
2) Draw down a tenon from the fullering, drive it into the hardie hole and check that it fits smoothly, both ways round. Cut off.
3) Fit into the hardie hole and upset to give the required width. Reheat and drive in a piece of the required diameter bar.
4) Grind the ends of the swage, upset by the bar, and smooth any sharp edges to finish the tool.

15 MORE TOOLS

Once your basic workshop is established, there are more tools that might be considered to add capability and enable you to work more quickly and efficiently. As a tiny part of a large metalworking industry, blacksmiths benefit from the availability of second-hand tools and equipment. A machine that is considered past its best for high-precision work may be ideal in the smithing shop. Even today, most industrial equipment is built to withstand heavy, continuous use and a lot of wear and tear. So it should continue to work well, with the kind of intermittent use it receives in a blacksmithing shop.

The following are tools that all find a place in a blacksmithing workshop. Only you can decide whether you really need one. As with most equipment, there is a considerable element of interaction and self-support. One machine can be used more effectively if another is available to help make the tools for it. If you have a welder, you almost certainly need an angle grinder to prepare and clean off welds.

Installation is an aspect not to be overlooked. The machine needs to be offloaded and moved into the workshop, sometimes onto substantial foundations. Electric power requirements need consideration. Most industrial equipment runs on three-phase power that can be expensive to install, if it is not already available. Many machines can either be run from a phase converter that takes in single-phase current and puts out three phase, or can be adapted by replacing the motor with a single-phase unit.

Power hammers, and in particular air hammers can be difficult, since the motor draws a large starting current under the heavy load of compressing air. Phase converters will not cope very happily with this, so a large single-phase motor and special switchgear may be required. Spring hammers have a clutch, so the motor starts without load, which may make them a better option.

Finally, before buying an expensive machine you are not sure you will use very often, there are two other possibilities to consider. Can you use the tool in someone else's workshop? Blacksmiths are helpful people. If you have friends, and provided you pay your way, they may be quite happy for you to spend a day using their piece of equipment. Alternatively, pay a local workshop to do the particular job. Many jobbing workshops exist by undertaking small pieces of work, and are only too happy to machine an item, bend tube or bar, drill a particularly large hole, or weld together your components.

POWER HAMMER

This is perhaps the most aspirational tool for a blacksmith. Much of the development of contemporary blacksmithing has been stimulated by the availability of power hammers. They provide a means of drawing down, spreading and generally changing the section of bars, very quickly and precisely. They can work material of a size that is beyond the capacity of a smith to forge by hand and in design terms, open up possibilities that are different in quality from hand hammering, or would otherwise be just too physically daunting to contemplate. It is

OPPOSITE PAGE: Detail of 'Market Column', by the author. Three sets of letters spelling the word 'Market', together with images of animals and fruit, were welded together to make a 5m (16ft 5in) high, sculptural marker, flagging the entrance to Leicester Market.

beyond the scope of this book to deal with the detailed use of a power hammer, but the following points are worth making.

Power hammers consist of a heavy cast-iron or fabricated steel frame, supporting the operating mechanism and hammer head over the anvil, so that the head strikes vertically down. Small hammers usually have an integral anvil, so the shock of the impact is contained within the frame. Larger hammers have an anvil that passes through a hole in the base of the frame, to be supported by a separate foundation.

A small power hammer.

The hammer is operated by a foot lever, or treadle, that controls the blow. A hand lever may also be fitted to operate the hammer for some purposes. Because the thickness of the work forged between the hammer head and anvil will vary, the drive to the hammer head cannot be a solid mechanical linkage. There must be some give in the system. The two fundamental

types of hammer solve this problem in different ways. One uses a spring system between the motor drive and the hammer head, the other places the hammer head at the end of a piston, pushed up and down a cylinder by compressed air.

Power hammers are rated in kilos or pounds, which is the weight of the ram and hammer 'head' that delivers the blow. A small hammer might be rated at 20kg (50lb), so its effect is considerably greater than even a large sledgehammer. A large power hammer might be rated at 225kg (500lb). With all hammers, the head is a removable steel tool block or pallet, driven down onto a similar tool fitted to the anvil. Both tools are substantial, hardened steel blocks, secured by wedges, so that they can be changed as necessary. These tools correspond in form and function to the head of a hand hammer. Thus there are plain flat-faced tools and fullering tools with convex faces, echoing a cross-pein hammer. A great deal can be achieved with just these, but many other special tools are available, or are made by the smith.

Smaller power hammers lend themselves to quick and easy tool changing, but with larger hammers this becomes impractical because of the sheer scale and weight of the tools. So these tend to be used with plain flat tools that can strike the metal directly, or drive a large variety of hand tools, often held by an assistant.

The hammer can only strike vertical blows, so control of the forging is achieved by manipulation of the bar between the tools. The fact that the top and bottom tools are in alignment means that, for example, shoulders may be forged on the top and bottom face of a bar very easily, and a tenon may similarly be drawn down by turning the bar through 90 degrees.

Long tapers can be drawn between fullering tools, the available length of heat being the only limitation. To take full advantage of this capability a gas or oil forge comes into its own by providing long heats, allowing a long taper to be drawn in one heat. Making the same taper using a coal or coke forge may need several separate heats. Using fullering tools end on, allows metal to be spread to a surprising extent. For example, a piece of 16mm (⅝in) or 20mm (¾in) round bar can be spread to provide the width of material for a small coal shovel or ladle. If a hammer is available in the workshop you will find it useful for almost every forging job, irrespective of size.

A power hammer is a wonderfully adaptable and tireless universal forging tool. But it is expensive, noisy, needs a substantial foundation and its products are only as good as the person using it.

FLY PRESS

A fly press happily has no power requirements, but depending on its size, may need to be bolted to the floor. It is essentially a screw press, not unlike a huge 'G' clamp. It has a cast-iron bed, integral with an open frame that guides a vertical

ram, operated by the screw. The screw is brought down by rotating a horizontal arm at the top of the machine that carries heavy ball weights to add inertia. There is usually a vertical handle extending down from the arm that gives convenient control to the movement of the ram. The vertical travel of the ram is controlled by an adjustable stop, enabling the same movement to be accurately repeated.

The virtue of the fly press is the pressure it can exert and its essential simplicity. The ram has a central hole into which the shank of a top tool can be secured, and the bed has 'T' slots to allow bottom tools to be bolted in place. Very simple tools can be made or improvised to bend, press, punch or shear metal. The press is an invaluable tool for a multitude of repetition tasks and the material can be worked hot or cold. Because of the way it works, the operator is also able to feel the movement of the metal, enabling the press to be used with sensitivity to, for example, straighten a heavy bar.

Tools can be tack welded together from odd scraps of bar, to bend metal hot or cold. Very large bends or rings can be made cold between a round bar top tool and two round bars as a bottom tool. Once the stop on the ram is adjusted, only one particular radius of bend will fit between the top and bottom tools, so several similar curves can be accurately

A selection of chestnut roasting ladles, by Alan Evans. These were all drawn down and spread under a small power hammer.

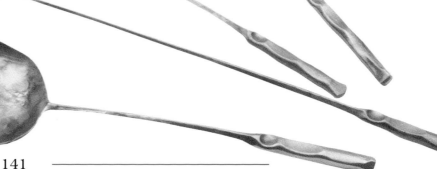

Making a complex bend in one operation under a large fly press. To make this possible, it is essential to have a gas forge capable of heating some 700mm (2ft 3in) of metal. In this way, seventy-two bars were bent in a morning.

reproduced. Elaborate, shaped top and bottom tools can also be constructed to form complex bends in one heat.

A large press can do small work, but a small one will not cope with large work. Fly presses are identified by a rather arcane numbering system, the larger the number, the bigger the press. They are also made in a standard pattern, or with a deep throat, enabling larger tools and workpieces to be accommodated. So if space and finances permit, buy a number 6 or 8, deep throat. The condition of second-hand machines is easy to inspect and although they are relatively expensive they can be good value.

WELDING EQUIPMENT

Gas and electric welding offer many advantages in the workshop, enabling metal to be joined in a wide variety of ways for particular purposes. Welding creates a joint by melting the parent metal and fusing it with additional weld metal from a wire or rod. The composition of the wire or rod is carefully formulated and must be compatible with the metal being welded. Welding is a skill and like forging takes time to learn.

Good welding handbooks are available and many colleges and evening institutes offer classes that deal in detail with safety issues and the particular skills of each process.

Gas Welding

Oxyacetylene equipment is of value in a blacksmithing workshop, not so much for welding but as a means of cutting and heating. An oxyacetylene welding torch will conveniently weld thin sheet metal up to perhaps 3mm (⅛in) thick, but is not really appropriate for thicker material. Electric welding then comes into its own. A gas weld is made by melting the edges of the joint with a torch flame and introducing weld metal from a thin wire rod held in the other hand. Tinted welding goggles are necessary.

Separate torches are available for welding, cutting or heating. Or a single torch body can be bought that accepts welding, cutting and heating attachments. Changing from one to another is quick, easy and effective. Nozzles of different sizes will be needed for each function to cope with different metal thicknesses.

Safety

In Britain, the gas cylinders cannot be bought, and must be rented. Reducer valves are fitted to the cylinders and for safety, flash-back arrester valves should also be fitted. Non-return valves in the hose connections are an additional safety measure. Cylinders are best secured on a trolley, enabling the equipment to be moved around the workshop.

Particular hazards in a blacksmithing workshop are, for example, damaging the reducer valves on the top of the cylinders by hitting them with the end of a piece of bar, or dropping hot metal and burning through gas hoses lying on the floor. The hoses should always be wound up over the cylinders, or the trolley, immediately after use and never allowed to lie around on the floor. Cylinders should never be stored or used without support. They could be knocked over and the brass valve stem sheared off, releasing high-pressure gas. The suppliers publish comprehensive safety procedures on the use and storage of inflammable gases, and the danger of high-pressure cylinders.

Gas Heating

If you work alone, a very useful piece of equipment is an economizer valve. This has a short arm on which the torch may be hung, the weight of the torch serving to shut off the gas. The unit is attached to the trolley or the wall, if the cylinders are in a fixed position. When the torch is picked up, the gas flows and the flame can be lit from a small pilot light on the body of the economizer. In use, this means that once the flame has been adjusted on the torch, it may be used, extinguished and relit repeatedly without needing to readjust the torch settings. It also means that after heating, say a rivet, instead of perching a lighted torch dangerously on the bench or wasting time turning it off, it can be hooked on the economizer while you are using a hammer.

The temperature of an oxygen and acetylene flame is well over 3,000°C, so the torch is a very useful means of providing local heat, making many processes, such as bending and twisting, far easier. The intensity of the flame means that a small part of a bar can be raised to red heat before the heat spreads very far. Oxy-propane can also be very useful for this purpose, but the flame temperature is some 500°C lower, so the heat tends to extend further. (Propane cylinders, on the other hand, do not have to be rented, so unless you want to weld, both heating and cutting can be achieved more economically using oxy-propane.) Heat can be applied with a welding torch, cutting torch or heating torch, taking care not to use the torch too close to the metal surface, to avoid melting or burning.

Gas Cutting (Flame Cutting)

It is a great asset to have a torch available for cutting metal. It provides a means of roughly cutting bars to length and more particularly, profiling steel plate to any desired shape. Plate from 3mm (⅛in) thickness and upwards can be conveniently cut, thicker plate being easier. The thicker the plate, the higher is the required oxygen pressure. So make sure that you have a reducer valve capable of delivering higher pressures. Cutting with a torch is primarily used for mild steel. Stainless steels and non-ferrous metals cannot be cut in this way. The torch may be simply hand held, but radius guides and wheel attachments are available, or fences and guides can be improvised to provide a smoother cut. A certain amount of slag usually adheres to the bottom edge of the cut, and needs chipping away with a chisel. But with care a reasonably clean edge can be produced, needing only a little grinding to finish.

Gas cutting steel plate at an outdoor blacksmithing event.

The cutting action produces a spray of flame and metal particles, for which reason it is usual to cut downwards, so that the sparks impact safely on the floor. Take care that you wear safety goggles and gloves, and ensure that the cuffs of your trousers are over the top of your boots. It is all too easy to shoot sparks down the side of a boot, or even through the eyelet holes. It is also easy to inadvertently cut tools, materials or the table under the plate.

Gas cutting is offered as a service by profile cutting firms that can cut plate of all thicknesses, neatly and accurately to your drawing.

PLASMA CUTTING

Plasma cutting can cut metal sheet and plate, ranging from very thin sheet metal – that cannot reliably be cut with a gas torch – up to plate perhaps 10mm (⅜in) thick. The torch is connected to a transformer and a gas or compressed air supply. An arc is produced in the head of the torch through which passes the compressed air or gas. The effect of this is to produce a superheated gas stream or plasma that exits the torch through a fine jet, vaporizing a cut though the metal. The cut is narrow in width and cleaner than that produced by gas cutting, leaving only a small 'burr' that can be easily ground off. The process has the great advantage that it is not limited to mild steel.

The plasma torch is much lighter and smaller than a gas cutting torch and the heat is so intense and localized that it can be guided by a hardboard or timber template. It offers a more flexible means of profiling thinner plate and sheet, in a variety of metals. Since metal vapour is given off, care must be taken to wear a suitable face mask, particularly when cutting non-ferrous metals. The machine also needs a gas or compressed air supply. This need be little more than a small compressor of the type you might use to spray paint, but it is nevertheless an additional consideration.

ELECTRIC WELDING

There is a bewildering variety of electric welding equipment available. Sets are now being produced to meet a DIY market. Which is to say that they are built down to a price and a little caution should be exercised when choosing new equipment. Second-hand, ex-industrial machines can be a better option. Larger welding sets may be three-phase, so choose with care.

Fundamentally all arc-welding systems work by transforming mains voltage, reducing it to perhaps sixty volts, too low a voltage to be too harmful. At the same time the amperage is considerably increased, using a

16mm (⅝in) steel plate letter shapes, produced by a profile cutting firm to the author's drawings. The edges of the letters were heated with a torch and hammered all round to upset a lip, creating shadows and highlights.

variable control on the machine. The arc is produced by a low voltage, high amperage spark, jumping the gap between the electrode and the workpiece. This produces intense local heat, causing the metal to melt.

Electric arc welding requires the right body-covering protective clothing, a helmet with the appropriate dark glass filter, and gloves. Filter glass units are available that darken electronically, the instant the arc is struck, and are adjustable to different degrees of shade. They are expensive, but replace a number of different tinted glass filters and are very convenient to use. The flash from all forms of arc welding produces ultraviolet and infrared radiation that can damage eyes and burn skin. The exposure of a bare arm for just a minute or two can cause burning similar to severe sunburn. Even in hot weather, cover up. A T-shirt is not sufficient protection. A long-sleeved cotton shirt makes all the difference. Various gloves are sold for different types of welding, but all should cover the wrists.

MMA (Manual Metal Arc)

This is the oldest form of hand electric welding, often simply known as 'arc' or 'stick' welding, since it uses short-coated rods or sticks of fairly thick wire to provide the weld metal. Arc welding sets can be either air-, or oil-cooled. Air-cooled sets are much lighter, more portable and cheaper, but their output can be variable, particularly when used for extended periods. They can be useful for small amounts of welding, and their portability enables welds to be made on site, at the end of a single-phase extension lead. Oil-cooled sets are heavier, but more robust and provide a steadier, better controlled arc.

Welding rods of different diameters are sold in packs. The thicker the rod, the higher the amperage needed to use it. An arc is struck between the end of the rod and the work, melting the joint and transferring molten metal from the rod as it is consumed. The rods are coated with chemicals

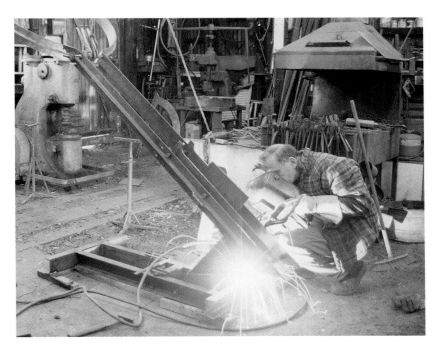

that help stabilize the arc, insulate the length of the rod and melt to create a slag coating, that prevents oxidation of the weld metal. The slag coating must be chipped and wire-brushed off the finished weld, which can take a little time. Different rods are available to weld a wide range of metals.

This kind of welding is probably the best type to buy initially. Compared with other systems, even oil-cooled sets are relatively cheap. They will run effectively on a single-phase supply, and can provide all the welding you might need for blacksmithing purposes. Their advantage is simplicity and flexibility. They can be used both indoors and out; with the right rods they will weld a variety of metals, and the small diameter of the rod enables welds to be achieved in awkward places, through holes for example. They are excellent for welding bar and plate, but not really suitable for welding thin sheet steel, despite being advertised in car magazines. MMA welding requires some skill. There are many books on the subject, and welding classes are available in many colleges and evening institutes.

Arc welding a large sundial in the workshop.

MIG (Metal Inert Gas)

This is a more elaborate system that uses thin, bare welding wire from a reel, driven by a small motor through a long flexible tube to the torch. The feed to the torch also contains a hose, supplying inert gas from a cylinder. A trigger on the torch controls both the wire feed and the gas. Controls on the machine housing set the current and other variables. Adjusted correctly, the same machine may be used to weld both thin sheet metal, or heavy steel plate. An arc is struck between the tip of the weld wire and the work, melting the wire and the joint that are protected from oxidation by the inert gas stream. The wire is fed continuously as the tip melts away. Substantial weights of metal can be deposited quickly and easily, almost like icing a cake.

MIG welding has the advantage of speed, several times that of stick welding. Since the wire is not coated, there is no slag to chip off the weld, although a certain amount of 'spatter' can be produced, leaving particles of metal to be scraped or brushed away. It is easier than MMA to weld uphill, or in awkward positions. The system can be operated with one hand, so components can be held together with the other and tacked in place. With all the correct adjustments it is a very effective, easy and clean system. But because of its speed, care must be taken with settings. Metal is deposited very quickly, and may build up on the surface without penetrating to make an effective joint. However, if the weld metal is penetrating and fusing properly, MIG is a very good way of building up metal to fill gaps or restore profiles.

MIG is a more expensive system than MMA, not simply in the initial cost but in the rental and refill costs of shielding gas cylinders. These contain argon and carbon dioxide mixtures that are relatively expensive. The size of the torch can limit access to narrow spaces, and since the welding wire is pushed through its sheathing to the torch, there is a limit to its length, so the welding machine itself must always be fairly close. Because the quality of the weld depends on an effective gas shield, MIG welding can encounter problems out-of-doors and be impossible in windy conditions. The cost of reels of wire can represent a larger outlay than a pack of stick welding rods, and the wire can rust over a period of time, causing the feed to jam in the machine.

TIG (Tungsten Inert Gas)

This combines many of the advantages of gas and arc welding. The torch contains a tungsten electrode with a similar gas shielding system to a MIG welding torch, but employing pure argon gas rather than argon mixtures. The arc is struck between the electrode and the work, melting the joint and the weld metal, which is introduced from a thin rod, held in the other hand like a gas welding rod. The tungsten electrode is not essentially consumed but does need to be sharpened every so often. TIG welders have very fine control of the weld current, enabling the same machine to output just a few amps or a hundred or two, allowing both thin sheet metal or thicker bar and plate to be welded.

Newer machines do not have a large transformer, but use an inverter system to control the current. This means that quite a powerful machine can be small in size and relatively portable. Some machines have sophisticated electronic controls, enabling various welding settings to be programmed, stored in a memory and called up for particular applications.

TIG welding is slower than MIG, being similar in speed to gas welding. But it is very clean, produces no spatter, penetrates well and is very adaptable. Since it provides an intense heat source, some welds may be made by fusion alone, without using a welding rod. A wide variety of metals can be welded. These include mild and carbon steels, stainless steel, copper and copper alloys. If the machine has alternating current output, it can also weld aluminium.

This is the most expensive type of welding machine. The pure argon shielding gas is also more expensive than the argon mixtures used for MIG welding. It does, however provide very clean, smooth, precise welds in a variety of metals and over a wide range of thicknesses.

BENCH DRILL

A facility to drill holes hardly needs much explanation. A good bench or floor standing drill allows holes to be made neatly and accurately. If it has a tilting table, holes can be drilled into the workpiece at a precise range of angles, and awkward pieces of work can be secured more easily. An adjustable stop on the quill of the drill controls its travel, so blind holes can be drilled to a predetermined depth.

A 13mm or ½in chuck is important, since this allows the use of stepped shank drills that will give a drilling capacity up to 25mm (1in) diameter. A good range of speeds are also important, more particularly the slower speeds for drilling metal. In general a second-hand industrial machine is likely to be better value than a new DIY model, for the same price. With belt-driven drills, it is relatively easy to substitute a three-phase motor with single-phase motor, if necessary.

There are safety considerations to do with clamping workpieces and avoiding loose hair or clothing being caught round the chuck, all of which is dealt with in books on machine shop practice. These also contain details of cutting speeds, lubrication and other considerations.

POWER HACKSAW OR CUT-OFF SAW

A power saw is very helpful simply to cut lengths of bar material. A gas cutting torch, angle grinder or hacksaw can be useful ways of cutting bar stock, but a power saw is more precise and consistent.

A power hacksaw can also be cutting metal while you are doing something else.

A hacksaw has a reciprocating blade, while a cut-off saw has a rotating, circular blade. Both secure the metal in a vice that may be set to an angle as well as making right-angle cuts. They also usually have a feed for cutting oil, to lubricate the blade, and very importantly a bar attachment with stops, which can be set to allow a number of pieces to be accurately cut to the same length. The siting of these tools is important, since a 6m length of stock bar may need to be fed into the vice.

LATHE

A lathe might seem to be a needlessly precise luxury in a blacksmithing workshop, and it is by no means essential, but there are pieces of work that can be achieved so much more easily if one is available. It can be used to make tools for the fly press, drill accurate holes, machine pins and fittings, precise tenons on the end of bars, or a journal bearing for a gate hinge. As with many tools, if you have a lathe available you will find uses for it that you never anticipated.

Again, small work may be undertaken on a large lathe, but large work cannot be done on a small one. If you should need to machine bearings to pivot a gate, the diameter that will pass through the headstock spindle is the critical dimension. There are many books dealing with machine shop practice that describe in detail the use of lathes.

BENCH GRINDER

A bench grinder is useful for a multitude of maintenance jobs in the workshop. It can be used to sharpen drills, chisels, punches, lathe tools, TIG welding electrodes, centre punches, scribers and so on. A small grinder is cheap to buy, and will pay for itself in keeping good cutting edges on tools.

16 ASSEMBLY AND FINISHING

A good solid piece of plate provides a flat surface on which smaller items can be assembled. This will need to be perhaps 25mm (1in) thick or more. A large engineer's square can be used to ensure that verticals are truly vertical and small, odd ends of bar can be saved for use as packing pieces to provide horizontal surfaces, on which components can be set, parallel with the plate. The components can be clamped to the plate, or it can be drilled allowing bolt fixings to be used. Larger structures like gates or grilles are usually assembled on trestles. Two or more of these can be positioned on the workshop floor and levelled with a spirit level, then levelled to each other to provide a horizontal surface on which components can be placed (*see* page 19).

Logic and care are needed to work out the sequence of assembly. Some items can be put together very easily since the components support each other. Others may start as a precarious collection of bits that only attain stability when they are all joined together. These are often the hardest to hold, to check or to weld. Pushing them into soft soil or a bucket of sand can sometimes be an answer.

ADJUSTING AND FITTING

It is at the assembly stage that any inaccuracies in the components will be revealed and necessary adjustments can be made before they are finally joined. Where possible, components should be temporarily assembled using clamps, binding wire, or nuts and bolts through rivet holes. If surfaces or edges do not line up correctly they can be filed or ground, or the part can be bent or twisted until it fits.

It is far better to adjust individual components than to begin assembly with the idea that if there are any discrepancies, they will all be taken up when the last joint is pulled together and secured. Because of the flexibility of the material, structures can often be sprung or drawn together to make a fit. But care is needed to avoid building some distortion into the whole structure in the process. In some instances, components can be securely joined at one point and a torch used to heat the free ends to bring them into line. A torch can also be used, after all the joints have been finished, to make adjustments to small details.

Where joints are to be riveted, it is good practice to check that the holes are clear and fit in line. If the faces of the holes are not true, setting the rivet may pull the components out of line. So, if necessary, file or grind the mating surfaces. It may be necessary to pass a drill or a round file through the hole to clear it and ensure alignment. If a joint is secured with a pattern of rivets, it is better to mark out and drill one part, then use this as a jig to drill the other. The parts must be securely clamped together while drilling. The alternative of marking out and drilling each part separately calls for a great deal of precision. So avoid making life needlessly difficult.

AVOIDING DISTORTION

Even after care has been taken to ensure a good fit between parts, the act of making

OPPOSITE PAGE: Gilded, hammer-textured details on a gate by the author. The black surface is burnished graphite paint.

the joint can, in itself, have some effect on the geometry of the structure. Welding tends to pull the joint, hot wrapping can bend a bar by drawing pieces together, the impact of setting rivets or riveting the end of a tenon can disturb the relationship of components, and so on. It is therefore very important to check the structure throughout the assembly process and be immediately aware of any distortion. A large square is essential to check frame structures like gates and screens. Checking the dimensions of frames across the diagonals is also useful. As a general principle, it is always better to try and balance any movement of the metal by completing joints alternately at one side or end, then the other. It is never a good idea to just start at one end and keep going.

For this reason it is conventional welding practice to connect a whole structure with 'tack' welds, before beginning to weld each joint solidly. Tacks should be no larger than necessary; big enough to hold the parts together, but small enough to avoid putting too much heat into the structure and causing distortion. Tack welding serves precisely the same purpose as tacking stitches used by a dressmaker to hold the parts of a garment together in preparation for seaming. Even after tacking, the structure can be distorted, unless care is taken to plan a balanced sequence of welds. There are many methods used to minimize distortion that are dealt with in specialist welding handbooks.

A lot of distortion can be eliminated by careful clamping. But using powerful clamps to hold components together does not in itself avoid the distortion caused by the heat of welding or the heat used to wrap joints or heat rivets. However, introducing diagonal bracing pieces clamped onto the structure to hold it square, can be well worthwhile. This is a good way to maintain the geometry of the frame of a gate or screen, while tenons are being riveted. Cutting loose spacers to fit between

bars may similarly serve to prevent them being pulled together by the action of hot wrapping a joint.

Whether a structure is large or small, it needs good support to allow rivets to be set, or tenons riveted. 'Backing up' is essential to allow the rivet to be hit hard enough to upset it and make a good fixing.

MARKING COMPONENTS AND PLANNING ASSEMBLY

Mark corresponding components with numbers, letters, or centre punch marks for assembly, don't rely on chalk marks. With all the care in the world they still disappear. Punch marks can often be placed where the joint itself will cover them. For example on the tenon and the inner face of the mortise, or on bars where they will be covered by collars or wrapped joints. If marks cannot be completely obscured, try to place them behind or underneath.

Planning the sequence of assembly is important. A gate or screen laid on trestles should not be turned over while it is still vulnerable to distortion. Plan to work from the side that allows the most effective fixings to be completed first, then turn it over. When the trestles are laid out in the first place, try to anticipate the clearance necessary to provide access for all the fixing processes and position them appropriately. It is annoying to discover that when riveting a tenon, the hammer hits the wall on the back swing.

FINISHING

Despite all that forging, the surface of the metalwork is the only bit you see, so it deserves careful treatment. Good finishing takes time. Many well-made pieces of work are ruined by poor, unthinking finishing. Treacly lacquer or paint, or even matt paint do very little for the work. Hot forging produces surface marks and textures that are part of the character of the work and can be camouflaged by poor finishing. Just the action of the fire can texture the metal. At the very least, the finish should seek to preserve the appearance of the forged metal. At its best, it should enhance it.

Where possible, components should be cleaned to some degree before assembly. A vigorous wire brushing, or better still a wire brush on an angle grinder, will remove much of the loose scale and burnish the surface. Small components can be pickled in proprietary phosphoric acids solutions to remove the oxide completely. Or parts may be shot or sandblasted. Even if during assembly the components are heated to weld, wrap or rivet joints, prior cleaning is worthwhile since the heat from a torch is localized, and only a little work is needed to remove its effects.

Wax Finishing

If the item is to be used in a dry, indoor environment, it can be wax-finished. The metal may be highlighted first, by cutting back through the black oxide surface with abrasive paper, to give emphasis to edges and develop the forged texture. The item can then be treated with two or three coats of wax, allowing them to dry thoroughly

A steel bowl by the author that has been kept at red heat in a coke fire for some fifteen minutes, the oxide removed by pickling and the surface waxed.

between applications. If a darker surface is required, a coat of proprietary graphite, wax polish (grate polish) can be used directly on the metal, followed by waxing. This is effective over the surfaces left by acid pickling, or blast treatment and restores the black oxide appearance. It is better to dilute graphite wax with white spirit, or cellulose thinners to enable it to be brushed on. It is quicker to apply this way and avoids the tendency of the graphite to cake on the surface.

An alternative is to use rust as a decorative finish. Left to itself, steel will develop rust in spots and patches, but with special preparation it can be made to rust evenly, producing a rich orange brown surface, like a suede shoe. The metal should be shot or sandblasted to strip the oxide and leave the bare steel chemically clean. It should then be hung or stood where it can be sprayed evenly with water containing a little ammonium chloride, maybe a teaspoonful to a pint of water. A garden insecticide sprayer is ideal. The surface should be dampened periodically, without creating runs and dribbles. If the liquid forms pools on the metal these areas will blacken, so mop them up. Within a few hours the metal will be rusted. It is better to build up the rust, let it dry, then brush it with a clean (not oily) wire hand brush. The metal can then be re-wetted with the solution until the rust is even. Finally rinse with plenty of clean water, dry thoroughly and wax.

Plain wax is better thinned out with white spirit. If the wax is carefully heated and melted, white spirit can be added to produce a thin, brushable paste. Brushing enables wax to be applied to textured surfaces more easily and it can also be driven into gaps and cavities. The wax should be allowed to dry and buffed with a soft cloth before recoating. 'Renaissance wax' is a recipe used by museum conservators, for it provides a hard and inert protective coating. It consists of four parts by weight of microcrystalline wax, to one part of polythene 'A'

wax. The two waxes are carefully melted in a pan and at least the same volume of white spirit added to make a paste that is thin enough to be brushable when cool. Failing this, silicone furniture wax can be used, similarly diluted and brushed on.

Blacksmiths traditionally used beeswax, often applying it as a block to the still hot metal, so that it melted over the surface. Over time this will produce a golden brown colour on bright areas of the metal. This can be attractive, but is in fact the result of breakdown products in the wax attacking the steel and causing fine rusting under the wax surface.

In many interior environments, a wax finish will be very effective in preserving the metal, particularly if the owner can be persuaded to wax the piece regularly. In other situations, despite initial waxing, a fine and often localized film of rust can develop. This is more likely if the metal is fairly thick. Temperature changes can cause condensation to form on the metal surface and rusting develops. Items on cool window ledges, in kitchens, or worse still in bathrooms are prone to this problem. Regular waxing is probably a domestic chore belonging to a bygone age, but in some situations it may be the only answer.

Clear lacquers for metal are also available, for brushing, air spraying, or in aerosol packs, that might give better protection in these situations. These are available with glossy or matt finishes. But they never seem to have the depth and subtlety of a waxed surface. An initial coat of matt sprayed lacquer, followed by waxing to give the sheen, is probably the best compromise. Lacquers are also difficult when they eventually do break down. Inevitably in the end, areas chip, flake or scratch, allowing odd little rust spots to develop.

Painting
In Britain, waxing or lacquering metalwork offers little protection outdoors, so external metalwork must, at the very least,

be painted. The effectiveness of a paint finish depends on good preparation. Heavy forge scale left on the metal can eventually flake off, taking the paint with it. So cleaning back to bare metal is essential. Using a rotary wire brush on an angle grinder can go a long way to achieving this, if it is done with care. But this is not as effective as acid pickling or shot blasting. Blast cleaning is available as a service, and is listed in the Yellow Pages. The cost of having, say, a gate shot-blasted, will be repaid if the maintenance over a few years is considered.

Shot-blasted steel surfaces will begin to rust very quickly if left exposed. In damp weather this can be happen within a few hours, so metal primer paint should be brushed or sprayed on as soon as possible. For small objects the aerosol primer paints sold for car refinishing can save time and trouble, and can be overcoated with conventional household spirit-based paints. Complete coverage is important, so an undercoat should be applied before the finishing coat of paint.

Eggshell or satin finishes seem to suit the forged surface better than matt or high gloss. A finish much used by smiths is a black with a little fine flake graphite mixed in, perhaps a teaspoonful or two to every 500ml of paint ready for spraying. It is important that the graphite be 'flake' not amorphous. This is obtainable in small quantities from locksmiths. The paint is applied by spray or brush and just before it is touch dry, a hand, or a lint-free cloth can be used to burnish the surface, exposing the graphite. If the paint is simply left to dry, it will exhibit no trace of graphite whatever. This paint has the great virtue that it mimics the appearance of the burnished and waxed black oxide finish. It also allows areas to be highlighted by burnishing, to develop the surface texture of the metal.

Highlighting may also be achieved by dragging a fairly dry brush with a lighter paint over the already painted surface. Silver paint can be dragged over black, for example. The paint may also be applied by dabbing with a balled up cloth or a piece of foam plastic. In a similar fashion another colour can be brushed or sprayed over the base colour and immediately wiped with a balled up cloth to leave it just in the crevices.

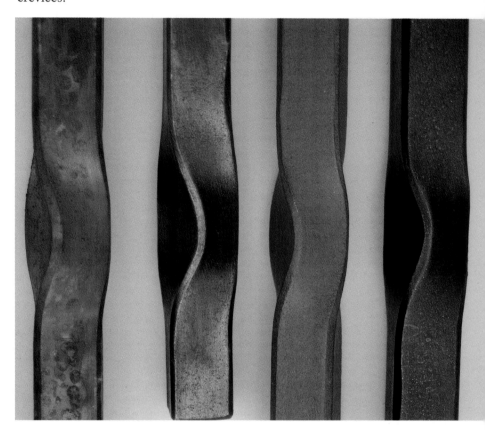

Because they are slightly porous, satin and eggshell paints provide less protection than gloss. It is therefore a good idea to use gloss paint as an undercoat to a satin finish for external use.

Gilding

Gilding has traditionally been used to enhance areas of metalwork. It brings a wonderful richness and contrast, and can be used to highlight areas of heavy texture. It is available in two basic forms as 'loose' or 'transfer' leaf. Transfer leaf is far easier

Finish samples. (Left to right) The oxide surface after heating; the oxide surface after wire brushing and waxing; the bar shot-blasted, rusted and waxed; the bar shot-blasted, zinc sprayed and finish-painted with burnished black graphite paint.

to use. The gilding is usually applied over the final paint finish. The area to be gilded is brush-painted with a special lacquer called 'gold size'. When this is almost dry, the leaf is applied and burnished into place, sticking it to the size. Transfer leaf is laminated to a tissue paper backing that makes it simpler to handle.

Gold leaf is available in a variety of colours and carat values. A carat is a twenty-fourth part, so pure or 'fine' gold is 24 carats. The higher the carat value, the less the risk of tarnish. Gold is alloyed with other metals to make it redder or greener. Despite its apparent delicacy, so long as the gilded surface is not subject to abrasion, it is remarkably durable, even in very exposed exterior situations. The leaf and gold size may be bought from specialist art material suppliers.

Zinc Spraying and Galvanizing

The climate in Britain provides ideal conditions for rusting, as anyone who has owned a car can testify. So more substantial treatments are advisable to provide corrosion protection for external metalwork. Zinc spraying or hot dip galvanizing both provide coatings of zinc metal that protect steel from rusting. Metal-finishing firms offer these as services. The virtue of zinc coating is that it makes subsequent paint finishes largely cosmetic. If the paint becomes chipped, the metal will still not rust, since the zinc coating gives protection.

Zinc spraying is often undertaken by firms who do shot-blasting and cleaning. The metal is blast-cleaned with steel shot, to strip rust and oxide, and key the surface. The molten zinc is then sprayed on within a short space of time, before any re-rusting or contamination occurs. Zinc spraying gives a slightly granular coating and is normally primed with a special etch primer that keys to the zinc. Conventional paint finishes can then be used to provide the decorative finish. The granular surface is not evident after painting. Since it is hand-sprayed, the process is as good as the operator and spray will in any case not penetrate into joints or crevices. This problem may be countered by using zinc-rich paint on these internal surfaces before or during assembly. The only limit to the size of work that can be treated, is the size of the booth used for shot-blasting and spraying.

Hot dip galvanizing is a more mechanized operation, in that the work is completely immersed in an acid bath to strip rust and oxide, and chemically clean the surface, before immersion in a tank of molten zinc. When the metalwork is withdrawn, a zinc coating is left on the surface. This process has the virtue that zinc can, to some degree, penetrate crevices or will seal them. Internal surfaces will also be coated so long as cavities are vented and there are no air traps. On the face of it, hot dip galvanizing would seem to be the perfect solution, and done well it probably is. But handled badly, drips, runs and spikes of zinc can be left on the metal and, worse still, there is a risk of the structure distorting in the heat of the process. The size of the zinc bath limits the size of work that can be treated.

With both processes it is important to speak to the people involved so that you know what they can do and they know what you want. Zinc spray firms will also usually be able to prime and paint the work at a reasonable additional cost. Galvanizing gives the metal a crystalline zinc surface that does not take paint well. It must either be left to weather, to provide a key for the paint, or it must be treated with a solution to etch the surface. This is a preparation called 'T' wash, that is brushed or sprayed on, left until the surface blackens and then washed off. It may then be painted in the normal way. In Germany it is apparently contemporary practice to install architectural metalwork in a galvanized state, then return six months later to brush-paint it.

FURTHER READING

BLACKSMITHING TECHNIQUE

Andrews, Jack, *New Edge of the Anvil* (Skipjack Press, 1994).
Bealer, Alex W, *The Art of Blacksmithing* (Castle Books, 1995).
The Blacksmith's Craft (The Countryside Agency, 1997).
Lillico, J.W., *The Blacksmith's Manual* (The Countryside Agency, 1991).
Weygers, Alexander G., *The Complete Modern Blacksmith* (Ten Speed Press, 1997).
Wrought Ironwork (The Countryside Agency, 1997).

CONTEMPORARY BLACKSMITHING

Chatwin, Amina, *Into the New Iron Age* (Coach House Publishing, 1995).
Lucie-Smith, Edward, *The Art of Albert Paley* (Harry N. Abrams, 1996).

BLACKSMITHING HISTORY

Campbell, Marian, *Decorative Ironwork* (V&A Publications, 1997).
D'Allmagne, H.R., *Decorative Antique Ironwork* (Dover Publications, 1968).
Menten, Theodore, *Art Nouveau Decorative Ironwork* (Dover Publications, 1981).
Martinie, Henri, *Art Deco Ornamental Ironwork* (Dover Publications, 1995).
Geerlings, Gerald K., *Wrought Iron in Architecture* (Dover Publications, 1983).

WELDING

Davies, A.C., *The Science and Practice of Welding* (Cambridge University Press, 1996).
Pritchard, Derek, *Soldering, Brazing and Welding* (The Crowood Press, 1996).
Vause, W.A., *The Art of Welding* (Nexus, 1999).

GENERAL

Street, Arthur & William Alexander, *Metals in the Service of Man* (Penguin, 1998).

GLOSSARY

Alloy a mixture of two or more metals, or of metal and non-metallic elements.

Anneal heating steel to red heat and allowing it to cool slowly to leave it in its softest state.

Anvil the iron or steel block on which the blacksmith forges hot metal.

Anvil tools tools with a square shank to fit the hardie hole of the anvil. These include hardies, fullers and swages.

Bick or beak the horn or pointed end of the anvil.

Bolster a tool consisting of a heavy plate pierced with a hole or holes to support a hot metal workpiece, while a hole is punched or drifted through it.

Butcher a special set chisel of concave form, sharpened on one face, designed to notch the corners of square bar to make a tenon.

Centre punch a short punch with a sharp pointed end, used to make impressions in metal to locate the point of a drill, or mark a position for punching.

Clip *see* Collar.

Cold chisel a chisel designed to cut cold metal. Shorter and with a less acute cutting edge than a hot chisel.

Collar a flat metal band fitting round two or more adjoining bars to make a connection.

Cone mandrel a conical cast iron former, offering a variety of diameters over which bars may be forged to make bends and rings.

Drawing down tapering a bar.

Drift a tool driven through a punched hole to modify or refine its shape.

Farrier a blacksmith who specializes in shoeing horses.

Flatter a set tool with a wide flat face, used to flatten and smooth surfaces.

Forge verb: to work hot steel with a hammer; noun : both the fire used to heat the metal and the workshop in which this takes place.

Former a workshop-made tool, over which a workpiece can be bent or shaped.

Fuller a steel tool with a blunt convex end, usually driven by a sledgehammer, to make grooves or spread hot metal. Bottom fullers fit the hardie hole. Top fullers have a rod or timber handle.

Fullering the act of using a fuller. Spreading metal.

Hand hammer a hammer for use in one hand.

Hardening heat treating steel to harden it, usually for toolmaking purposes.

Hardie a short chisel that fits in the hardie hole of the anvil.

Hardie hole the square hole through the face of the anvil, designed to accept the shank of the hardie and other tools.

Hot chisel a steel chisel designed to cut hot metal. More slender and with a more acutely ground cutting edge than a cold chisel.

Hot set a chisel with a handle for cutting hot metal.

Jig strictly, a device that holds the work and guides a tool, but commonly applied to any special tool over which the metal is shaped to produce repeat components.

Jumping up forging part of a bar back into itself in order to thicken it.

Mandrel	a bar over which metal is wrapped or forged.
Monkey tool	a short steel tool driven with a hand hammer that is used to fit over a roughly forged tenon to refine its shape and square the shoulder.
Mortise	a hole in a bar or component designed to receive a tenon.
Pein	the opposite end of the hammer head to the face.
Pritchel hole	the round hole in an anvil over which a farrier punches the square nail holes in horseshoes, using a special punch called a pritchel.
Punch	a hardened steel tool used to make holes or marks.
Quench	abruptly cooling hot metal in oil or water.
Rodded tools	set tools wrapped with steel rod to provide a handle.
Scarf	the shaped, angled end of a bar prepared for fire welding.
Scroll wrench	a wrench consisting of two fingers projecting at right-angles to a handle used for bending bars.
Sets	any tool set on a handle, for striking with a sledgehammer.
Set hammer	a round- or flat-faced hammer for striking with a sledgehammer.
Sledgehammer or Sledge	a heavy hammer intended for use with two hands.
Shafted tools	set tools punched with a hole and fitted with a timber handle.
Swage	a concave steel tool used to shape or support hot metal. Bottom swages fit the hardie hole. Top swages have a rod or timber handle.
Swage block	a large cast-iron block pierced with shaped holes and swage grooves around its edge. Used for supporting and shaping hot metal.
Swaging	the act of using a swage.
Tap and die	engineering tools used to cut screw threads. The tap cuts internal threads and the die cuts external threads.
Tapering	forging a bar to progressively reduce its section, drawing down.
Tapping	cutting an internal thread.
Tempering	reducing the dead hardness of steel quenched from red heat, in order to soften it to the required degree of toughness.
Tenon	a projection usually forged on the end of a bar to fit a mortise hole to make a fixing.
Top and bottom tools	swages and fullers that can be used in matched pairs, one fitted in the anvil, the other held by the smith and struck with a sledgehammer.
Upsetting	jumping up, forging part of a bar back into itself in order to thicken it.
Wrapping	winding a red hot bar around another bar or bars, to create a joint.

INDEX